T0104167

ON THIS DAY

in HISTORY

BUSHEL
& PECK
BOOKS

Bushel & Peck Books is dedicated to fighting illiteracy all over the world.
For every book we sell, we donate one to a child in need——book for book.
To nominate a school or organization to receive free books,
please visit www.bushelandpeckbooks.com.

Type set in Josefin Sans, Prater Script Pro, Cheap Pine Sans, and Scrapbook Basic.

LCCN: TBD
ISBN: 9781638192008

First Edition

Printed in the United States

10 9 8 7 6 5 4 3 2 1

ON THIS DAY

in HISTORY

A KID'S DAY-BY-DAY GUIDE TO **2,675** SIGNIFICANT EVENTS

Christin Farley

JANUARY 1

Ellis Island in 1919

1962 The Navy SEALs special operations force begins.

1908 New York City's Times Square celebrates its first New Year's Eve with the ball drop.

1863 Slavery is abolished in the U.S. with the Emancipation Proclamation signed by President Abraham Lincoln.

1892 The gateway to the U.S., Ellis Island, opens as an immigration station.

1999 Eleven European nations adopt the euro as their currency.

1902 University of Michigan beats Stanford in the first-ever Rose Bowl game in Pasadena, California.

1913 The US Postal Service delivers its first packages (no longer only letters!).

1986 Mandates for seatbelts in the U.S. take effect.

 # JANUARY 2

1947 In India, Mahatma Gandhi begins his nonviolent march for peace.

1788 Georgia becomes the fourth state to join the Union.

1839 The first photo of the moon is taken by inventor and photographer Louis Daguerre.

1910 Berkley, California, opens the nation's first junior high school.

1890 Alice Sanger becomes the first female White House staffer.

1906 The world's first air conditioner receives a US patent thanks to inventor Willis Carrier.

1929 U.S. and Canada partner to preserve Niagara Falls.

1944 The British Atlantic Patrol uses the first helicopter in warfare.

📑 JANUARY 3

1987 Music legend Aretha Franklin is inducted into the Rock and Roll Hall of Fame as its first female artist.

1777 General George Washington defeats British forces at the Battle of Princeton, New Jersey, in the Revolutionary War.

1870 Construction begins on the Brooklyn Bridge in New York.

1959 Alaska becomes the forty-nineth state to join the Union.

1977 Steve Wozniak and Steve Jobs incorporate Apple Computers.

1988 Ice hockey great Wayne Gretzky becomes the youngest player to score 700 goals in NHL history.

2018 The world's first bionic hand, with touch sensation for wear outside of a lab, debuts in Rome.

2022 The world's oldest living person, Kane Tanaka, turns 119.

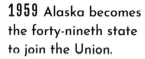

📑 JANUARY 4

Elvis Presley

JAN
FEB
MAR
APR

MAY

JUN

JUL

AUG

SEP
OCT
NOV
DEC

1754 Columbia University begins and is first known as King's College.

1863 James Plimpton of New York patents four-wheeled roller skates.

1865 The first permanent headquarters are opened for the New York Stock Exchange near Wall Street in New York City.

1920 The National Negro Baseball League organizes as the first Black baseball league.

1954 In Memphis, Tennessee, Elvis Presley records his first demo for Sun Records.

1958 Spaceship Sputnik 1 re-enters Earth's atmosphere from space, only to burn up.

1962 New York City runs its first automated subway train.

JAN

2004 NASA rover *Spirit* makes a successful landing on Mars.

 # JANUARY 5

1903 The first telegraph cable from San Francisco to Hawaii opens for public use.

1914 Henry Ford of Ford Motors announces its minimum per-day wage of five dollars, which doubles most workers' pay.

1931 Lucille Thomas becomes the first woman to purchase a baseball team: the Topeka, Kansas, franchise.

1957 Baseball legend Jackie Robinson announces his retirement.

1836 Famous frontiersman Davy

The Alamo (still standing today)

Crocket arrives in Texas to aid in the Battle of the Alamo.

1859 The first steamboat launches on the Red River.

1943 US sports teams agree to a later start of season due to World War II.

 # JANUARY 6

1898 Simon Lake, a US naval engineer, sends the first telephone message from a submerged submarine.

1907 Montessori schools begin, with Maria Montessori opening her first in Rome.

1914 Merrill Lynch stock brokerage firm begins operations.

1929 Catholic missionary Mother Teressa arrives in Calcutta to begin her life's humanitarian work.

1942 The first commercial flight around the world is scheduled by Pan American Airlines.

1975 Pat Sajak and Vanna White make their *Wheel*

 JAN
FEB
MAR
APR
MAY
JUN
JUL
AUG
SEP
OCT
NOV
DEC

of *Fortune* debut on NBC-TV.

2016 North American box office record is broken with *Star Wars: The Force Awakens.*

2021 "Stop the Steal" supporters storm the US capitol building.

📑 JANUARY 7

1785 Jean Pierre Blanchard and John Jeffries fly the first balloon across the English Channel.

1890 The fountain pen, invented by African American William Purvis, receives a patent.

1927 The famous basketball trick-shot team, the Harlem Globetrotters, play their first game in Illinois.

1944 The Bell P-59 becomes the first US fighter jet.

1969 US Congress doubles the yearly salary of the US president.

1991 Iraqi President Saddam Hussein prepares his troops for war with the U.S. (Gulf War).

1994 Tonya Harding wins the US female

Figure Skating Championship.

1999 Impeachment trial begins for US President Bill Clinton.

Bill and Hillary Clinton in 1994

 # JANUARY 8

1942 Stephen Hawking, one of the world's most brilliant theoretical physicists, is born.

1675 - New York Fishing Company becomes America's first commercial corporation.

1833 Boston Academy of Music becomes America's first music school.

1937 San Jacinto, Nevada, sets the state record for coldest temperature at -50°F.

1956 Elvis Presley's *Don't Be Cruel* and

FEB
MAR
APR
MAY
JUN
JUL
AUG
SEP
OCT
NOV
DEC

Hound Dog songs stay at the top of the charts as number one for eleven weeks.

1974 The price of gold in London hits a record high of $126.50 an ounce.

1992 US President George W. Bush meets with the Japanese prime minister, only to become ill and throw up on him. Yikes!

2018 Cost of US national disasters in 2017 is announced as $306 billion.

JANUARY 9

1788 Connecticut becomes the fifth state to join the Union.

1861 Leading up to the Civil War, Mississippi secedes from the Union.

1965 *Beatles '65* album hits #1 on the charts, where it stays for nine weeks.

1984 Van Halen releases their most successful album, entitled *1984*.

2000 Harrison Ford and Julia Roberts win the 26th People's Choice Awards.

JAN

2002 Artist of the Century is awarded to Michael Jackson at the American Music Awards.

2007 Apple co-founder Steve Jobs announces the iPhone.

1811 Scotland hosts the first women's golf tournament.

 # JANUARY 10

Thomas Paine

1776 Thomas Paine, a political philosopher, publishes his fifty-page pamphlet called *Common Sense* in support of the American Revolution.

1946 For the first time, radar signals bouncing off the moon are detected by scientists.

JAN

FEB

MAR

APR

MAY

JUN

JUL

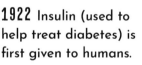
AUG

SEP

OCT

NOV

DEC

1924 Max Roach, a famous American percussionist, is born in North Carolina.

1863 London's first underground railway opens from Paddington to Farringdon.

1985 Lenny Wilkens, coach of the Seattle Supersonics, becomes first to coach in 1,000 games.

1997 "Entertainment Tonight" airs its 4,000th episode.

2004 Critic's Choice awards Best Film to *The Lord of the Rings: The Return of the King.*

2022 The US Mint commemorates the life of poet Maya Angelou on quarter coins.

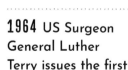 # JANUARY 11

1922 Insulin (used to help treat diabetes) is first given to humans.

1964 US Surgeon General Luther Terry issues the first government report on the hazards of smoking.

2010 A massive 7.0 earthquake strikes off the coast of Haiti, its most destructive quake ever.

Amelia Earhart in 1936

1935 Amelia Earhart makes the first solo flight from Hawaii to California.

1755 Alexander Hamilton, one of the America's Founding Fathers, is born.

1973 Baseball's American League adopts the "designated hitter" rule.

2007 In Edinburgh, Scotland, author J.K. Rowling finishes her seventh Harry Potter novel.

 # JANUARY 12

1939 Publisher Martin Goodman founds Marvel Comics (previously Timely Comics) in New York.

1948 The United Kingdom opens its first supermarket.

1906 The committee on football rules

FEB
MAR
APR
MAY
JUN
JUL
AUG
SEP
OCT
NOV
DEC

JAN
FEB
MAR
APR
MAY
JUN
JUL
AUG
SEP
OCT
NOV
DEC

decides to legalize the forward pass.

1908 The Eiffel Tower sends its first long-distance radio message.

2004 The RMS *Queen Mary 2* takes its maiden voyage as the world's largest ocean liner.

1959 Berry Gordy Jr. establishes Motown Records (originally Tamla Records) in Detroit.

1773 Charleston, South Carolina, opens the country's first public museum.

1998 Nineteen European countries agree to ban human cloning.

The RMS Queen Mary 2

 JANUARY 13

1930 Mickey Mouse appears in his own comic strip.

1901 The first Texas oil field is discovered near Beaumont.

1957 Frisbee production begins.

2012 The cruise ship *Costa Concordia* sinks off the Italian coast.

1942 The Ford Motor Company obtains a patent to manufacture plastic cars (since World War II causes metal shortages).

1999 Basketball legend Michael Jordan announces his retirement from the NBA for the second time.

1943 Adolph Hitler declares "total war" against the Allies during World War II.

1978 NASA selects its first women astronauts, Sally Ride among them.

 # JANUARY 14

1952 The National Broadcasting Company (NBC) launches the *Today* show.

 JAN
 FEB
 MAR
 APR
 MAY
 JUN
 JUL
 AUG
 SEP
 OCT
NOV
DEC

JAN
 FEB
MAR
APR
MAY
JUN
 JUL
AUG
SEP
OCT
 NOV
 DEC

1981 The US-Iran hostage crisis comes to an end.

1943 Franklin Roosevelt becomes the first US President to cross the ocean by plane.

1967 Sonny & Cher release their music single *Beat Goes On*.

1979 Martin Luther King Jr.'s birthday is first recognized as a national holiday.

1990 *America's Funniest Home Videos* debuts on ABC.

2020 Ken Jennings wins *Jeopardy's* "The Greatest of All Time" tournament.

1878 Britain's Queen Victoria receives a demonstration of the telephone from inventor Alexander Graham Bell.

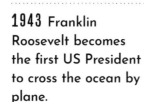 # JANUARY 15

1909 A funeral procession includes an automobile hearse for the first time.

2009 US Airways Flight 1549 crashes into the Hudson River (amazingly, there are no fatalities).

The Pentagon

1967 Los Angeles hosts the very first Superbowl.

1943 The Pentagon becomes the nation's largest office building.

1870 The Democratic party is first characterized by a donkey in *Harper's Weekly*.

1861 Inventor Elisha Otis of Vermont patents the steam elevator.

1961 Diana Ross and the Supremes sign with Motown Records.

1975 Space Mountain welcomes its first riders at Disneyland.

 # JANUARY 16

2009 The largest bank in the nation, Bank of America, is bailed out with billions of dollars in government aid.

 JUN
 JUL
 AUG
 DEC
FEB
MAR
APR
MAY
SEP
OCT
NOV

1991 The start of the Persian Gulf War.

2017 The last person to walk on the moon, Astronaut Eugene Cernan, passes away.

1938 Benny Goodman and his band perform the first jazz concert in Carnegie Hall.

1493 Christopher Columbus sails back to Spain from the New World.

1868 William Davis, of Detroit, patents the refrigerator car.

1939 *Superman* comic strip debuts in the *Daily* paper.

2019 Golden State Warrior standout Stephen Curry makes NBA history, hitting eight or more three-point field goals in three consecutive games.

Christopher Columbus in a 1519 painting.

 JANUARY 17

1949 The first Volkswagen Beetle cars arrive from Germany.

1994 One of the largest US earthquakes, measuring 6.6 on the Richter scale, hits Los Angeles.

1871 Andrew Smith Hallidie patents the first cable car.

1929 Old time cartoon *Popeye* make its comic strip debut.

2008 Famous grandmaster chess player, Bobby Fischer, dies at age sixty-four.

1942 Professional boxer Muhammad Ali is born in Louisville, Kentucky.

2012 LeBron James sets NBA record as the youngest player in history to score 20,000 career points.

1917 Denmark sells the Virgin Islands of St. Thomas, St. John, and St. Croix to U.S. for $25 million.

 # JANUARY 18

1930 The Beatles make it onto the US Billboard Hot 100 for the first time.

 JAN
 FEB
 MAR
 APR
 MAY
 JUN
 JUL
 AUG
 SEP
OCT
 NOV
DEC

JAN

FEB

MAR

APR

MAY

JUN

JUL

AUG

SEP

OCT

NOV

DEC

1773 Boston exhibits the first polar bear in America.

1896 The University of Iowa hosts the first college basketball game with five players on each side.

1911 An aircraft lands on a ship's flight deck for the first time.

2005 France reveals the Airbus A380, the world's largest commercial aircraft.

2010 Canadian recording artist Justin Bieber releases his *Baby* single.

1882 A.A. Milne, creator of Winnie-the-Pooh, is born in London.

1903 The first successful radio transmission is sent from the U.S. to Europe.

JANUARY 19

1977 Miami receives snow for the first time!

1955 The first-ever televised presidential press conference is held by US President Eisenhower.

1903 France announces its first

Tour de France bicycle race.

....

1922 A geological survey claims that within twenty years, the US oil supply will be depleted.

....

1955 The board game "Scrabble" debuts in Britain and Australia.

....

2013 Cyclist Lance Armstrong admits to cheating in all seven of his Tour de France victories.

....

2013 NASA's rover *Curiosity* finds calcium deposits on Mars.

....

1993 First Pixar film, *Toy Story*, begins production.

....

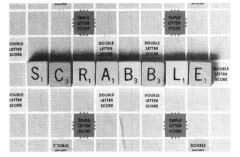

Scrabble game

📄 JANUARY 20

1937 US presidential inaugurations move to January 20th from March 4th.

....

JAN

FEB

MAR

APR

MAY

JUN

JUL

AUG

SEP

OCT

NOV

DEC

1945 Franklin D. Roosevelt begins his fourth term as US president.

2006 Disney Channel releases the TV movie *High School Musical*.

1996 Michelle Kwan wins the US Female Figure Skating Championship.

1981 William Maclure publishes America's first book on geology.

1930 American astronaut Buzz Aldrin is born in New Jersey.

1998 Eagles and The Mamas and Papas join the Rock and Roll Hall of Fame.

📑 JANUARY 21

1799 Edward Jenner introduces the smallpox vaccine.

1905 Fashion designer Christian Dior is born in France.

Depiction of Edward Jenner administering the smallpox vaccine in 1796

1972 New York City holds the first *Star Trek* convention.

1984 Scott Hamilton wins the US Male Figure Skating Championship.

1987 Blues musician B.B. King donates his collection of 7,000 recordings to the University of Mississippi.

1798 The first novel is published in America: *The Power of Symphony* by William Hill Brown.

1903 Escape artist Harry Houdini escapes from a police station in Amsterdam.

1921 Agatha Christie, British crime writer, publishes her first novel.

 # JANUARY 22

1973 US Supreme Court issues its ruling on *Roe v Wade* case.

2021 Baseball legend Hank Aaron dies at age eighty-six.

1990 Dr. Suess publishes his last book, *Oh, the Places You'll Go.*

2020 Covid-19 outbreak places 100 million people on

JAN
FEB
MAR
APR
MAY
JUN
JUL
AUG
SEP
OCT
NOV
DEC

lockdown in Wuhan, China.

1964 The world's largest cheese, weighing 34,591 pounds, is manufactured for the New York's World Fair.

1985 Ninety percent of Florida's citrus crop is damaged

by unusually cold weather.

1988 Mike Tyson beats Larry Holmes for the heavyweight boxing title.

2018 Netflix becomes the world's largest digital media and entertainment company.

 # JANUARY 23

1986 Rock and Roll Hall of Fame inducts Buddy Holly.

2009 President Obama orders the closure of US detention facility Guantanamo Bay.

1983 The first episode of *The A-Team* airs on NBC.

1909 For the first time, a morse code distress call leads to a sea rescue.

1789 Georgetown University begins

as the nation's first Catholic college.

1991 Embattled Iraqi forces in Kuwait cause the world's largest oil spill.

 # JANUARY 24

Entrance to Pixar Animation Studios

2006 Disney announces plans to purchase Pixar Animation Studios.

1975 Arizona hosts the world's first McDonald's drive-thru.

1848 Gold is discovered in Sutter's

Mill in Coloma, California, by James Marshall. The famous gold rush begins.

1940 Director John Ford release his film *The Grapes of Wrath*.

1950 The Brooklyn Dodgers sign Jackie

 JAN
 FEB
 MAR
 APR
 MAY
 JUN
 JUL
AUG
SEP
OCT
NOV
DEC

Robinson with a record contract of $35,000.

1978 Sweden becomes the first country to ban aerosol sprays.

2004 Robotic rover *Opportunity* lands on Mars.

1984 Steve Jobs introduces the Macintosh, Apple's new personal computer.

Steve Jobs in 2001

JANUARY 25

1961 Disney's *101 Dalmatians* opens in US theaters.

1949 The Emmys— awards for television

entertainment—are held for the first time.

1554 São Paulo, Brazil, becomes a city.

1840 American explorer Charles Wilkes identifies Antarctica as a new continent.

1959 American Airlines makes the first transcontinental commercial jet flight from Los Angeles to New York City.

2021 The US Senate confirms Janet Yellen as the first female secretary of the treasury.

 # JANUARY 26

1988 *The Phantom of the Opera* makes its debut on Broadway.

1965 India declares Hindi as its national language (over one hundred languages are spoken throughout the country).

1837 Michigan becomes the twenty-sixth state to join the Union.

2020 Kobe Bryant and daughter die in a helicopter crash.

2004 A decomposing sperm whale explodes in Taipei, Taiwan, while being transported for research.

1905 The world's largest diamond is

unearthed in South Africa (a whopping 3,106 carats!).

1958 Talk show host and comedian Ellen

DeGeneres is born in Louisiana.

1961 Hockey great Wayne Gretzky is born in Ontario, Canada.

JANUARY 27

2010 Apple Computers announces its tablet computer: the iPad.

1756 Wolfgang Amadeus Mozart, world-famous composer, is born in Austria.

1996 Germany observes the International Holocaust Remembrance Day for the first time.

1880 Thomas Edison patents the electric lamp.

1945 Auschwitz and Birkenau concentration camps are set free.

1951 A series of 126 nuclear tests begins at Nevada test site.

1956 Elvis Presley releases his first million-selling single, *Heartbreak Hotel*.

APR

MAY

JUN

JUL

AUG

SEP

OCT

NOV

 DEC

1888 The National Geographic Society begins in Washington, D.C.

 ## JANUARY 28

A vintage box of Legos

1958 Patent for Lego plastic bricks is filed in Denmark.

1915 US Congress establishes the US Coast Guard.

1813 Jane Austen's *Pride and Prejudice* publishes in Britain.

1887 Construction begins on the Eiffel Tower in Paris.

1913 Beverly Hills, California, becomes a city.

2017 Tennis twins Serena and Venus Williams compete for the Australian Women's Open.

FEB
MAR
APR
MAY
JUN
JUL
AUG

JAN

FEB

MAR

APR

MAY

JUN

JUL

AUG

SEP

OCT

NOV

DEC

1962 A women in Zimbabwe is stung 2,443 times by bees and survives, setting a world record.

2006 The Jonas Brothers promote their debut album on the "American Club" tour.

📑 JANUARY 29

1892 The Coca-Cola Company begins in Atlanta, Georgia.

1959 Disney's *Sleeping Beauty* opens in theaters.

1995 The San Francisco 49ers becomes the first team to win five Superbowl titles.

1954 American television personality Oprah Winfrey is born in Mississippi.

Oprah in 2014

1936 Babe Ruth joins baseball's Hall of Fame in New York.

Romeo and Juliet is performed for the first time.

1845 Edgar Allen Poe publishes his poem "The Raven."

2012 Shaun White, American snowboarder, receives the first perfect score for the superpipe.

1595 William Shakespeare's

 # JANUARY 30

1996 Magic Johnson returns to the LA Lakers after four years of retirement.

2020 World Health Organization declares the coronavirus a public health emergency.

1948 Mahatma Gandhi dies at age seventy-eight.

2010 Justin Bieber reaches one million Twitter followers.

1847 Yerba Buena, California, is officially renamed "San Francisco."

1933 Radio show *The Lone Ranger* begins its twenty-one-year run.

JAN

FEB

MAR

APR

MAY

JUN

JUL

AUG

SEP

OCT
NOV
DEC

JAN
 FEB
MAR
APR
MAY
JUN
JUL
AUG
SEP
OCT
NOV
 DEC

1933 Adolf Hitler becomes the chancellor of Germany.

1974 Actor Christian Bale is born in Wales.

 # JANUARY 31

1961 The first chimpanzee, named Ham, launches into space.

1942 Civilian car manufacturing stops in the US so factories can focus on military vehicles for World War II.

1950 US President Truman approves the construction of the hydrogen bomb.

1971 Apollo 14 launches on a mission to the moon.

1990 The first McDonald's in Russia opens in Moscow.

2014 The world's oldest flamingo, Greater, dies at age eighty-three in an Australian zoo.

2020 The United Kingdom leaves the European Union (Brexit).

2017 President Trump nominates Neil Gorsuch to the US Supreme Court.

FEBRUARY 1

1926 Black History Month is first observed in the U.S.

1992 Russia and the U.S. declare the official end of the Cold War.

1982 David Letterman's first episode of *Late Night* airs on TV.

1884 The first volumes of the Oxford English Dictionary are published.

1790 The U.S. holds its first session of the Supreme Court.

1972 Handheld scientific calculators hit the market for $395.

1978 Harriet Tubman is honored on a US postage stamp.

1994 English Singer Harry Styles is born.

Entrance to Late Show with David Letterman

JAN FEB MAR APR MAY JUN JUL AUG SEP OCT NOV DEC

JAN

FEB

MAR

APR

MAY

JUN

JUL

AUG

SEP

OCT

NOV

DEC

 # FEBRUARY 2

1887 Punxsutawney, Pennsylvania, celebrates the first Groundhog Day.

1653 New York City, formerly called New Amsterdam, becomes a city.

1848 The U.S. and Mexico sign the Treaty of Guadalupe Hidalgo, ending the Mexican-American War.

2019 Over forty mummies are unearthed at an ancient burial site in South Cairo, Egypt.

1935 The lie detector test, or polygraph, is first used in criminal investigations.

2021 Amazon founder, Jeff Bezos, steps down as CEO after 30 years.

1852 The world's first flushing toilets open to the public in London.

Jeff Bezos in 2019

FEBRUARY 3

1919 The League of Nations holds its first meeting.

1870 The US Constitution's Fifteenth Amendment grants African American men the right to vote.

1690 The American colonies issue their first money in Massachusetts.

1966 The first weather satellite is launched into orbit at Cape Canaveral, Florida.

1959 Music legend Buddy Holly dies in a plane crash.

1995 Eileen Collins of the U.S. becomes the first woman to pilot the space shuttle.

1894 Famous American illustrator Norman Rockwell is born.

1882 Circus showman P.T. Barnum purchases his world-famous elephant, Jumbo.

 # FEBRUARY 4

 JAN
 FEB
 MAR
 APR
 MAY
 JUN
 JUL
 AUG
 SEP
 OCT
 NOV
DEC

JAN

FEB

2004 Mark Zuckerberg founds Facebook.

1789 George Washington becomes the first US president.

1938 Disney releases *Snow White*.

1932 The U.S. hosts its first Winter Olympics in Lake Placid, New York.

2008 Thomas S. Monsoon is named the sixteenth president of the Church of Jesus Christ of Latter-day Saints.

1957 The electric typewriter hits the market for the first time in Syracuse, New York.

1993 The Boston Celtics hold "Larry Bird Night" at the Garden to celebrate his career.

FEBRUARY 5

1969 The population of the U.S. reaches 200 million.

1989 Kareem Abdul-Jabbar makes NBA history as the first player to score 38,000 points.

1870 Philadelphia hosts the first motion

A package of Jell-O mix

picture shown to a theater audience.

1918 Stephen W. Thompson becomes the first US pilot to down an enemy airplane.

1922 *Reader's Digest* publishes its first issue.

1953 Disney releases its newest animated film, *Peter Pan.*

1981 The largest-ever Jell-O mold, big enough to hold 9,246 gallons of Jell-O, is made in Brisbane, Australia.

1994 *Where on Earth Is Carmen Sandiego?* debuts on Fox TV.

 # FEBRUARY 6

1952 Queen Elizabeth II begins her reign over the United Kingdom and

other Commonwealth realms.

1935 The board game Monopoly hits the market for the first time.

1964 Jamaican-American musician Bob Marley is born.

1964 France and Britain agree to build the Channel Tunnel.

1971 The first golf ball is hit on the moon by Alan Shepard.

2014 *The Tonight Show* host Jay Leno airs his last show.

1911 US President Ronald Reagan is born in Illinois.

2018 SpaceX launches the world's most powerful rocket, the Falcon Heavy.

The SpaceX Falcon Heavy rocket at a launch in 2019

 FEBRUARY 7

2019 Baseball great Frank Robinson dies at age eighty-two.

1812 British novelist Charles Dickens is born in Chatham, England.

1964 Baskin-Robbins introduces "Beatle Nut" ice cream as Beatles mania sweeps the world.

2005 Ellen MacArthur surpasses the speed record for solo sailing around the world.

1984 Astronaut Robert L. Stewart takes the first untethered spacewalk.

1994 Whitney Houston wins the twenty-first American Music Awards.

2021 The Superbowl has its first female referee, Sarah Thomas.

1818 *Academician* magazine begins publication in New York City.

 # FEBRUARY 8

1910 The Boy Scouts of America begins.

1974 The US space station, Skylab, ends its operations.

1627 Explosives are first used in mining.

1922 The White House installs radio capabilities.

1928 Hartsdale, New York, receives the first transatlantic TV image.

1965 Diana Ross and the Supremes release *Stop in the Name of Love*.

2002 Winter Olympics open in Salt Lake City, Utah.

2018 Twitter reports a quarterly profit for the first time as a public company.

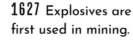

FEBRUARY 9

1943 In response to World War II, the U.S. begins to ration shoes to three pairs per person per year.

1871 US Congress authorizes an office for federal fish protection.

1932 The U.S. enters the Olympic two-man bobsled competition for the first time.

1964 The Beatles first appear on *The Ed Sullivan Show*.

The Beatles in 1964

1997 Debbie Reynolds wins American Comedy Award.

1997 *The Simpsons* becomes the longest-running animated series to date.

2020 British Airways Boeing 747-436 accidentally makes the fastest journey from New York to London.

1987 Actor Michael B. Jordan is born in Santa Ana, California.

 # FEBRUARY 10

2014 Child star Shirley Temple dies at age eighty-five.

1996 IBM's Deep Blue becomes the first computer to beat chess champ Gary Kasparov.

2005 Prince Charles of Wales announces

JAN
FEB
MAR
APR
MAY
JUN
JUL
AUG
SEP
OCT
NOV
DEC

engagement to Camilla Bowles.

. . . .

2009 US satellite "Iridium 33" and Russian satellite "Kosmos 2251" collide in space.

. . . .

1933 Postal Telegraph-Cable Company delivers the first singing telegram.

. . . .

1940 *Tom and Jerry* cartoon makes its debut.

. . . .

1989 *Miami Vice* airs its one-hundredth TV episode.

. . . .

2009 Amazon announces the production of the Kindle 2.

. . . .

FEBRUARY 11

1990 Political prisoner Nelson Mandela is released from prison after twenty-seven years

. . . .

1847 American inventor Thomas Edison is born in Milan, Ohio.

. . . .

2020 For only the second time in one hundred years, snow falls in Baghdad.

. . . .

2021 Sister Andre, the world's second-oldest person, turns 117.

. . . .

1878 The Boston Bicycle Club becomes

Julia Child on a US postage stamp

the first cycling club in the U.S.

The French Chef, premieres.

1942 *Archie* comic book debuts.

2020 Brazil's Maya Gabeira rides the largest wave ever surfed by a woman.

1963 Julia Child's cooking show,

 # FEBRUARY 12

1892 The birthday of President Abraham Lincoln becomes a national holiday.

1918 The National Association for the Advancement

of Colored People (NAACP) begins.

2017 Adele wins the Grammy Awards' Song of the Year for her song *Hello*.

JAN

FEB

MAR

APR

MAY

JUN

JUL

AUG

SEP

OCT

NOV

DEC

2019 According to US Treasury, the US national debt tops $22 trillion.

2019 After nearly one hundred years, rare black panthers are spotted in Kenya.

1924 The first presidential speech via radio is given by President Calvin Coolidge.

1870 Women gain the right to vote in Utah.

1878 Frederick Thayer receives a patent for the catcher's mask in baseball.

FEBRUARY 13

2000 The *Peanuts* comic strip has its last newspaper publication.

2021 Donald Trump is acquitted in a second Senate impeachment trial.

1795 The University of North Carolina opens as the nation's first state university.

1861 Abraham Lincoln becomes the sixteenth US president.

1866 Outlaw Jesse James robs his first bank in Liberty, Missouri.

Outlaw Jesse James around the 1870s

1968 10,500 additional US soldiers are sent to Vietnam.

1977 American Eric Heiden wins the nation's first world speed skating championship.

1994 Scottie Pippen receives the MVP award at the NBA All-Star game.

 # FEBRUARY 14

1962 Jacqueline Kennedy gives a televised White House tour.

1912 Arizona becomes the forty-eight state to join the Union.

1876 Alexander Graham Bell files a patent for the telephone.

1818 Frederick Douglass is born in Maryland.

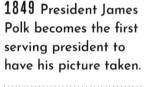

President James Polk

1849 President James Polk becomes the first serving president to have his picture taken.

1859 Oregon becomes the thirty-third state to join the Union.

1967 Aretha Franklin records her single *Respect*.

1992 Comedy *Wayne's World* opens in theaters.

📋 FEBRUARY 15

2003 Nearly thirty million people around the world protest against the war with Iraq.

1965 The maple leaf becomes the new symbol on Canada's national flag.

1965 American singer and television host

Nat King Cole dies at age forty-five.

1758 Mustard is advertised for the first time.

1903 Morris & Rose Michtom introduce America to the first teddy bear.

1943 J. Howard Miller produces the wartime propaganda poster "We Can Do It!"

1950 Disney's *Cinderella* premiers in Boston.

2016 Ed Sheeran wins Best Song and Taylor Swift wins Best Album at the 58th Grammy Awards.

 ## FEBRUARY 16

1900 The first daily Chinese newspaper is published in San Francisco.

1923 British archeologist Howard Carter opens the tomb of Egyptian pharaoh Tutankhamun ("King Tut").

1950 Long-time game show *What's My Line* debuts on CBS

1968 The first 9-1-1 emergency system

 JAN
 FEB
 MAR
 APR
 MAY
 JUN
 JUL
 AUG
 SEP
OCT
NOV
DEC

begins service in Haleyville, Alabama.

1992 LA Lakers retire the jersey of Magic Johnson.

2013 Soccer star Lionel Messi scores his three-hundredth goal for Barcelona.

1858 William Vanderburg and James Harvey patent the first ironing board.

1932 The first patent for a fruit tree is given to James Markham.

📑 FEBRUARY 17

1985 US postage for first-class stamps rise from 20 cents to 22 cents.

1934 State College, Pennsylvania, introduces the first high school driver's ed course.

2014 NBC hosts the premiere of The *Tonight Show Starring Jimmy Fallon.*

2020 Jeff Bezos pledges $10 billion to aid in fighting climate change.

1801 Thomas Jefferson is elected US president over Aaron Burr.

Michael Jordan in 2014

JAN
FEB
MAR
APR
MAY
JUN
JUL
AUG
SEP
OCT
NOV
DEC

1815 The War of 1812 ends when President James Madison signs the Treaty of Ghent.

1963 NBA legend Michael Jordan is born in Brooklyn, New York.

1913 Oregon begins the first US minimum-wage law.

 # FEBRUARY 18

1930 Astronomer Clyde Tombaugh discovers Pluto.

1885 Mark Twain's *Adventures of Huckleberry Finn* is first published in the U.S.

2001 NASCAR favorite Dale Earnhardt Sr. dies in the Dayton 500 race.

JAN

FEB

MAR

APR

MAY

JUN

JUL

AUG

SEP

OCT

NOV

DEC

Winston Churchill in 1941

1879 Statue of Liberty sculptor, Frederic-Auguste Bartholdi, receives a patent for his design.

1901 Winston Churchill delivers his first speech to the British House of Commons.

1972 California Supreme Court abolishes the death penalty.

1978 Oahu, Hawaii, hosts the first Ironman Triathlon competition.

2021 NASA successfully lands the *Perseverance* rover on Mars.

1987 Girls Scout executives change the uniform color from traditional green to blue.

 FEBRUARY 19

1906 Kellogg's company, known for its breakfast cereals, is founded.

1878 Thomas Edison patents his phonograph.

1913 Cracker Jack adds a prize to its boxes for the first time.

1985 Coca-Cola introduces Cherry Coke.

1968 The first teachers' strike is held in Florida.

2019 Bernie Sanders announces his second bid for president

2019 New York City places a ban on hair discrimination.

1968 PBS airs the debut of *Mister Rogers' Neighborhood*.

 # FEBRUARY 20

1962 John Glenn becomes the first American to orbit the Earth.

1972 Cleveland Cavaliers beat the New York Knicks for the first time.

1998 Olympic figure skater Tara Lipinski wins the gold medal.

 JAN
 FEB
 MAR
 APR
 MAY
JUN
JUL
AUG
SEP
OCT
NOV
DEC

2018 Venezuela becomes the world's first country to launch a virtual currency.

....

1943 The Paricutin volcano erupts, burying two villages in Michoacán, Mexico.

....

1902 Landscape photographer Ansel Adams is born in San Francisco.

....

2013 Estonia debuts the first electric car charging station network.

....

2016 A lock of John Lennon's hair sells for $35,000 at an auction in Dallas, Texas.

....

 # FEBRUARY 21

1885 The Washington Monument is dedicated in Washington, D.C.

....

1948 NASCAR begins in Daytona, Florida.

....

1902 Dr. Harvey Cushing performs the first brain operation in the U.S.

....

2005 *Avatar: The Last Airbender* debuts on Nickelodeon.

....

1853 The longest college basketball game is played with six overtimes!

....

1925 The *New Yorker* magazine begins publication.

2018 Billy Graham, an American evangelist, dies at age ninety-nine.

1842 John J. Greenough patents the sewing machine.

 # FEBRUARY 22

Johns Hopkins University in Baltimore, Maryland

1997 Scottish scientists announce the first successful adult mammal cloning.

1959 The first NASCAR Daytona 500 is won by Lee Petty.

1876 John Hopkins University opens its doors for the first time.

1889 North and South Dakota, Montana, and Washington all join the Union.

JAN
FEB
MAR
APR
MAY
JUN
JUL
AUG
SEP
OCT
NOV
DEC

1909 The first US fleet, the Great White Fleet, returns from circling the globe.

1732 George Washington is born in Westmoreland, Virginia.

1923 The first successful chinchilla farm in the U.S. opens in Los Angeles.

1935 Due to disrupted sleep, President Franklin Roosevelt announces that airplanes are no longer permitted to fly over the White House.

📑 FEBRUARY 23

1941 Dr. Glenn T. Seaborg discovers the chemical element plutonium.

1836 The Battle of the Alamo begins.

1870 Following the Civil War, Mississippi rejoins the U.S.

1896 Tootsie Roll candies are first sold in Brooklyn, New York.

1940 Disney's *Pinocchio* is released.

1903 Cuba leases Guantanamo Bay to the U.S.

1954 Polio vaccines are first given to children.

FEBRUARY 24

1993 Eric Clapton wins the Grammy Awards with the song *Tear in Heaven.*

1998 Queen Elizabeth II knights singer Elton John at Buckingham Palace.

2008 Cuban President Fidel Castro retires after over thirty years in office.

2011 Space Shuttle *Discovery* makes its final launch.

2020 Memorial service is held for NBA star Kobe Bryant at the Staples Center.

Fidel Castro in Cuba in 1989

1920 Adolph Hitler founds the Nazi Party in Munich, Germany.

1955 Steve Jobs is born in San Francisco, California.

FEBRUARY 25

2000 The first Amazon Go grocery store opens in Seattle, Washington.

1836 Samuel Colt patents his multi-shot revolver.

1901 US banker J.P. Morgan begins the United State Steel Corporation.

1913 The Sixteenth Amendment is ratified.

1862 Congress forms the US Bureau of Engraving and Printing.

1919 The first state gasoline tax starts in Oregon.

1994 Yankees shortstop Phil Rizzuto joins the Baseball Hall of Fame.

2018 Norway's Marit Bjoergen becomes the most successful winter Olympic athlete of all time with fifteen metals.

JAN
FEB
MAR
APR
MAY
JUN
JUL
AUG
SEP
OCT
NOV
DEC

The Grand Canyon

1919 The Grand Canyon becomes a national park.

1983 Michael Jackson's *Thriller* hits number one.

1930 Manhattan, New York, installs the first red and green traffic lights.

1933 The groundbreaking ceremony is held for the Golden Gate Bridge.

1929 Teton National Park is created in Wyoming.

1967 Mario Andretti wins his first and last Daytona 500 race.

2021 Hasbro toys announces a gender-neutral name change for Mr. Potato Head.

FEB

1863 President Lincoln establishes a single, national currency.

📑 FEBRUARY 27

1932 American actress Elizabeth Taylor is born in London.

2020 390 million light-years away, scientists observe the biggest explosion in the universe.

2019 The world's smallest baby, born at 9.45 ounces, leaves the hospital to go home.

1974 The first issue of *People* magazine is released.

1827 New Orleans celebrates its first Mardi Gras.

1996 Gameboy releases its first Pokémon game.

1814 Beethoven's *Symphony No. 8*

Ludwig van Beethoven

premieres in Vienna,
Austria.

FEBRUARY 28

1922 Egypt becomes an independent country.

1983 TV program M*A*S*H* airs its final episode.

1784 John Wesley charters the first Methodist church in the U.S.

1849 The first boatload of gold rush hopefuls from the East Coast arrives in San Francisco.

1953 The double-helix structure of DNA is discovered in a Cambridge University lab.

2013 For the first time in almost 600 years, a pope resigns (Benedict XVI).

1977 Marineland in Los Angeles announces the birth of the first killer whale born in captivity.

MARCH 1

1872 Yellowstone becomes the first national park in the world.

1969 Baseball legend Mickey Mantle announces his retirement.

1803 Ohio becomes the seventeenth state to join the Union

1867 Nebraska becomes the thirty-seventh state to join the Union.

1984 MAC cosmetics begins in Ontario, Canada.

1964 President John F. Kennedy establishes the Peace Corps.

1994 Popstar Justin Bieber is born in Ontario, Canada.

1936 Construction of the Hoover Dam is completed.

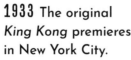

MARCH 2

1965 *The Sound of Music* premieres

1933 The original *King Kong* premieres in New York City.

1904 Theodor Seuss Geisel, aka Dr. Suess, is born in Springfield, Massachusetts.

2011 Steve Jobs announces the iPad 2.

2016 After 340 days aboard the International Space Station, astronaut Scott Kelly returns to earth.

1987 The median home price in the U.S. reaches about $100,000 for the first time.

1949 New Milford, Connecticut, welcomes the first automatic street lights.

1976 Walt Disney World hosts its fifty millionth guest.

Walt Disney World entrance in 2016

MARCH 3

1934 Congress adopts *The Star-Spangled Banner* as the national anthem.

 JAN
 FEB
 MAR
 APR
 MAY
 JUN
 JUL
 AUG
 SEP
 OCT
 NOV
DEC

1923 *Time*, a weekly magazine, is printed for the first time.

1845 Florida becomes the twenty-seventh state to join the Union.

2017 Nintendo releases the Switch videogame console.

1791 Congress establishes the US Mint.

2005 Steve Fossett becomes the first person to make a solo flight around the world without stopping.

1847 Inventor Alexander Graham Bell is born in Scotland

Alexander Graham Bell in 1913

 **MARCH 4**

1791 Vermont becomes the fourteenth state to join the Union.

....

1975 CBS airs the first *People's Choice Awards*.

....

1954 Dr. Joseph E. Murray performs the first successful kidney transplant.

....

1837 Chicago, Illinois, becomes a city.

....

1792 Hawaii is first introduced to oranges.

....

1975 Queen Elizabeth II knights comedic actor Charlie Chaplin.

....

1793 George Washington gives the shortest inauguration speech in history at just 133 words.

....

2012 Russia's Vladimir Putin wins presidential re-election.

....

MARCH 5

1982 Russian spacecraft *Venera 14* lands on Venus

....

1946 Winston Churchill, British prime minister, gives his famous "Iron Curtain" speech.

....

1750 The first Shakespearean play is performed in America.

....

JAN
 FEB
MAR
APR
MAY
JUN
JUL
AUG
SEP
OCT
NOV
DEC

1956 US Supreme Court bans segregation in schools.

1976 For the first time in history, the British pound falls below a $2 equivalent.

1998 NASA announces that the moon has enough water to support a human colony.

1770 The Boston Massacre takes place, leading up to the Revolutionary War.

 # MARCH 6

1899 Felix Hoffman patents Aspirin.

2012 A three-year-old McDonald's chicken nugget sells on eBay for $8,100.

1981 Iconic CBS anchorman Walter Cronkite retires from the *Evening News*.

1945 Gymnast George Nissan patents the first modern trampoline.

1970 The Beatles release their hit single *Let it Be* in the United Kingdom.

2018 The world's oldest message in a bottle—from 1886—is found in Western Australia.

2018 Amazon founder Jeff Bezos is named the world's richest person by *Forbes*.

2021 The US Senate passes the American Relief Plan, a COVID-19 relief bill amounting to $1.9 trillion in aid.

1836 The thirteen-day Battle of the Alamo ends in a victory for Mexico.

 # MARCH 7

1926 The first transatlantic phone call is made from London to New York.

1996 The Hubble Telescope releases its first surface pictures of Pluto.

The Hubble Telescope

JAN
FEB
MAR
APR
MAY
JUN
JUL
AUG
SEP
OCT
NOV
DEC

2016 Peyton Manning, of the Denver Broncos, announces his retirement.

2019 Britain's Queen Elizabeth II makes her first Instagram post.

1793 France declares war on Spain in the French Revolutionary War.

1969 Israel elects its first female prime minister.

 # MARCH 8

1969 Pontiac introduces its American muscle car, the Firebird Trans Am.

2014 Malaysian Airlines Flight MH370 goes missing with 227 passengers on board.

1975 The first celebration of International Women's Day is held.

1948 Religious instruction in public schools is ruled unconstitutional.

1999 Yankees legend Joe DiMaggio dies at age eighty-four.

201 South Dakota passes a law allowing teachers to be armed at school.

Joe DiMaggio on a US postage stamp

1894 New York enacts the first dog-license law.

1855 The first train crosses the railway suspension bridge at Niagara Falls.

MARCH 9

1959 Mattel introduces the first Barbie doll toy.

1820 Congress passes the Land Act, leading to westward US expansion.

1776 Philosopher Adam Smith publishes *The Wealth of Nations.*

1942 Construction begins on the Alaskan highway connecting Alaska to British Columbia.

1943 American chess legend Bobby Fischer is born.

1929 Eric Krenz becomes the first person to throw the discus beyond 160 feet.

1858 Albert Pott patents the first mailbox used by the US Postal Service.

 ## MARCH 10

1913 Abolitionist Harriet Tubman dies in New York at age ninety.

2021 Roblox video game platform goes public on the New York Stock Exchange.

1910 China officially abolishes slavery.

1864 Ulysses S. Grant is given command of the US Army.

1978 *The Incredible Hulk* with Bill Bixby premieres on CBS

2006 The *Mars Reconnaissance Orbiter* enters Mars's orbit to search for water.

APR

MAY

JUN

JUL

AUG

SEP

OCT

NOV

DEC

MARCH 11

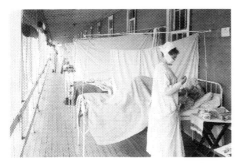

Flu ward during the Spanish Flu epidemic of 1918-1919

2011 A 9.0 earthquake (and soon-to-follow tsunami) strikes off the coast northeastern coast of Honshu, Japan.

. . . .

1892 Springfield, Massachusetts, holds the first public basketball game.

. . . .

1918 The first case of the Spanish Flu is confirmed in the U.S.

. . . .

1997 Queen Elizabeth II knights Paul McCartney of the Beatles.

. . . .

1961 To complement Barbie dolls, the Ken doll is introduced.

. . . .

1969 Levi Strauss adds bell-bottomed jeans to its clothing line.

. . . .

1959 Lorrain Handsbury becomes the first African American woman to have her play produced on Broadway.

. . . .

1930 William Taft becomes the first US president to be buried in Arlington National Cemetery.

📑 MARCH 12

1912 Oreo, the world's bestselling cookie brand, is first introduced.

1884 The state of Mississippi becomes the first to establish a state college for women.

1993 The first female US attorney general, Janet Reno, is sworn in.

1894 The first bottles of Coca-Cola are sold in Vicksburg, Mississippi.

1912 Juliette Gordon Low forms the first US Girls Scout troop.

Coca-Cola bottle designs through the ages

1948 American singer and guitarist James Taylor is born in Boston.

2008 Hulu's streaming service launches in the U.S.

2012 *The Hunger Games,* starring Jennifer Lawrence, premieres in Los Angeles.

📑 MARCH 13

1906 American suffragette Susan B. Anthony is born in Rochester, New York.

1781 William Herschel discovers the seventh planet from the Sun: Uranus.

1975 The first Chili's restaurant opens in Dallas, Texas.

2006 Construction begins on the 9/11 Memorial in New York City.

1519 Explorer Hernando Cortez lands in present-day Mexico.

2014 Marvel's *Captain America: The Winter Soldier* premieres in Los Angeles.

1877 Chester Greenwood invents

the earmuffs at age
fifteen.

 ## MARCH 14

1794 Eli Whitney patents the cotton gin.

2018 Students hold a nationwide walkout demanding action on gun violence.

1743 Faneuil Hall in Boston holds the nation's first town hall meeting.

2019 California declares it is drought-free for the first time in seven years

1879 Physicist Albert Einstein is born in Ulm, Germany.

1927 Warren Harding becomes the first US president to file an income tax report.

2006 After thirty-seven years as host, Mike Wallace retires from *60 Minutes*.

1942 K9 Corps begin training dogs for use in warfare.

 ## MARCH 15

1968 Jimi Hendrix is named "The Most Spectacular Guitarist in the World" by *LIFE* magazine.

....

1820 Maine biomes the twenty-third state to join the Union.

....

2019 As part of Fridays for Future, 1.5 million students participate in climate change protests around the world.

....

1933 Supreme Court Justice Ruth Bader Ginsburg is born in New York, New York.

....

1998 *Titanic* surpasses *Star Wars* to become the highest-grossing film in North America to date.

....

1892 New York introduces the automatic ballot voting machine.

....

1949 Four years of World War II clothes rationing ends in Britain.

....

Students participate in a Fridays for Future rally in 2019

JAN
 FEB
 MAR
 APR
 MAY
 JUN
JUL
AUG
SEP
OCT
 NOV
DEC

1955 US Air Force reveals the first self-guided missile.

MARCH 16

1621 American colonists meet the first Native Americans.

1913 US Navy launches the 15,000-pound battleship *Pennsylvania*.

1926 Professor and scientist Robert Goddard launches the first liquid-fueled rocket.

2006 US national debt reaches $9 trillion.

1802 West Point, the US military academy, begins in New York.

2010 Justin Bieber releases his single *U Smile*.

MARCH 17

1917 St. Louis, Missouri, hosts the nation's first women's bowling tournament.

461 Ireland's patron saint, St. Patrick, dies.

1737 Boston celebrates the nation's first St. Patrick's Day.

1930 Construction begins on the Empire State Building in New York.

2004 Spacecraft enters orbit around Mercury for the first time.

1968 Bee Gees, the British rock band, debuts on *The Ed Sullivan Show*.

2017 Disney's live-action remake of *Beauty and the Beast* opens in theaters.

1967 Charlie Brown and Snoopy from *Peanuts* appear on the cover of *LIFE* magazine.

1937 Amelia Earhart makes her first attempt at flying around the world.

A statue of St. Patrick

1917 American musician Nat King Cole is born in Montgomery, Alabama.

MARCH 18

1818 Barnum and Bailey open their first show in Madison Square Garden.

1662 Paris opens the first-ever public "bus" service.

1931 Schick razor brand reveals the first electric shaver.

1942 The US military begins its third draft for World War II.

1874 By treaty, Hawaii grants the U.S. excluding trading rights to the island.

1965 Soviet Alexey Leonov becomes the first person to walk in space.

1987 Gerber survey finds that the most popular baby names at the time are Jessica and Matthew.

MARCH 19

Pope Francis in 2019

MAR

1918 Congress approves daylight savings time in the U.S.

2003 The US war with Iraq begins with airstrikes on Baghdad.

1931 Nevada legalizes gambling to bring needed money to the state.

1953 The Academy Awards holds its first TV broadcast.

1990 Ottawa, Canada, holds the world's first women's ice hockey tournament.

1822 Boston officially incorporates as a city.

2013 Pope Francis begins his ministry as the 266th pope.

1977 *The Mary Tyler Moore Show* airs its last episode.

2020 Country music star Kenny Rogers dies at age eighty-one.

2019 The Walt Disney Company buys 21st Century Fox entertainment.

2020 NFL star Tom Brady moves to the Tampa Bay Buccaneers after twenty years with the New England Patriots.

1914 New Haven, Connecticut, holds the first international figure-skating tournament.

1990 The LA Lakers retire the jersey of #33, Kareem Abdul-Jabbar.

1999 Legoland officially opens in Carlsbad, California.

1963 New York City holds the first pop art exhibit.

1852 Author Harriet Beecher Stowe publishes her novel, *Uncle Tom's Cabin*.

MARCH 21

Alcatraz Island in San Francisco

1963 The US federal prison closes on Alcatraz Island in San Francisco.

1965 Martin Luther King Jr. begins his protest march from Selma to Montgomery, Alabama.

1904 Forrest Edward Mars Sr., the inventor of M&M candies, is born in Wadena, Minnesota.

1851 Lafayette Houghton Bunnell comes across California's Yosemite Valley.

2006 Twitter is founded, and co-founder Jack Dorsey sends the first "tweet."

2007 Apple releases its first Apple TV.

2019 For only the second time in history, Levi Strauss & Company is traded publicly on the New York Stock Exchange.

1952 The Cleveland Arena holds the first major rock and roll concert.

MARCH 22

1968 The first Red Lobster restaurant opens in Lakeland, Florida.

1457 The Gutenberg Bible is printed on a printing press, forever changing the way books will be manufactured.

1903 Due to drought, Niagara Falls runs out of water.

1934 Augusta, Georgia, hosts the first Masters golf championship.

1935 Iran becomes the official new name of Persia.

2018 Broadway opens the musical *Frozen*.

1931 *Star Trek*'s "Captain Kirk" (William Shatner) is born in Montreal, Canada.

2020 To curb COVID-19, India puts 1 billion people under daytime curfew.

MARCH 23

JAN
FEB
MAR
APR
MAY
JUN
JUL
AUG
SEP
OCT
NOV
DEC

A Wright plane in 1909

1998 *Titanic* wins eleven Oscars and the award for Best Picture at the Academy Awards.

1775 American revolutionary Patrick Henry makes his "Give Me Liberty or Give Me Death" speech.

1743 London premieres the first performance of Handel's *Messiah*.

1903 Orville and Wilbur Wright obtain an airplane patent.

1977 The final concert tour for Elvis Presley begins.

2001 Russian space station falls into the Pacific Ocean after reentering the atmosphere.

2011 Actress Elizabeth Taylor dies at age seventy-

nine in Los Angeles,
California.

  MARCH 24

1874 Harry Houdini,
the famous magician
and escape artist,
is born in Budapest,
Hungary.

1920 Morehead,
North Carolina, opens
the first US Coast
Guard air station.

2005 American
actress Sandra
Bullock receives her

Hollywood Walk of
Fame star.

1880 The first branch
of the Salvation Army
opens in New York.

2005 *The Office* TV
show premieres on
NBC.

1947 Congress
proposes limiting the
US presidency to two
terms only.

  MARCH 25

1668 The first horse
race in America takes
place in present-day

Long Island, New
York.

1954 RCA manufactures the first colored television.

. . . .

1996 A redesigned $100 bill, with additional security measures, begins circulation in the U.S.

. . . .

1947 British composer and singer Sir Elton John is born near London, England.

. . . .

1983 Michael Jackson first performs his "moonwalk" dance to a live audience.

. . . .

1863 Six US soldiers receive the first US Army Medals of Honor.

. . . .

2002 The reality TV show *The Bachelor* debuts on ABC.

. . . .

Elton John in 2015

 **MARCH 26**

1830 The first copy of the Book of Mormon is printed in Palmyra, New York.

. . . .

JAN
FEB
MAR
APR
MAY
JUN
JUL
AUG
SEP
OCT
NOV
DEC

2007 The US Postal Service reveals the design of the "Forever Stamp."

....

1982 Washington, D.C. holds a groundbreaking ceremony for the Vietnam Veterans Memorial.

....

1976 The first royal email is sent by Queen Elizabeth II.

....

1958 *Explorer III* becomes the third successful US Army satellite to launch.

....

1937 Farmers of spinach in Crystal City, TX erect a statue of Popeye

....

1926 America's first lip-reading tournament is held in Philadelphia.

....

1951 President Harry Truman adopts the design of the US Air Force flag.

....

 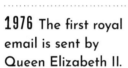 **MARCH 27**

1952 The comedic musical film *Singin' in the Rain* makes its premiere.

....

1912 The first cherry blossom trees are planted in Washington, D.C., a gift from Japan.

....

1933 Protestors gather in New York to show their disdain for Adolph Hitler.

1794 The US Congress authorizes the formation of the US Navy.

2007 Instant replay becomes a permanent officiating tool in the NFL.

1923 Jack O'Neill, the American surfer and creator of the wetsuit, is born in Denver, Colorado.

 # MARCH 28

1963 Alfred Hitchcock's movie *The Birds* is released.

1996 American author Stephen King publishes his book *The Green Mile*.

1799 New York abolishes slavery.

Alfred Hitchcock

JAN
FEB
MAR
APR
MAY
JUN
JUL
AUG
SEP
OCT
NOV
DEC

1990 President George Bush posthumously awards the Congressional Gold Medal to Jesse Owens.

2009 Swine flu officially makes its way to the U.S.

2017 The largest dinosaur footprint discovered to date is found in Kimberley, Australia.

1990 Michael Jordan scores a career-high of 69 points against the Cleveland Cavaliers.

1986 Singer and songwriter Lady Gaga is born in New York City.

MARCH 29

1638 Present-day Delaware is settled by Swedish colonists.

1951 The musical *The King and I* opens on Broadway.

1919 Ringling Brothers and Barnum & Bailey Circus merge.

1999 Wayne Gretzky, hockey phenomenon, scores the final goal of his NHL career.

A postage stamp illustration of a circus poster for Ringling Brothers and Barnum & Bailey

1812 The first wedding in the White House takes place.

2004 Ireland bans smoking in all workplaces, the first country to do so.

2019 Billie Eilish releases *When We All Fall Sleep, Where Do We Go?*, her first album.

1943 In response to World War II, the US begins rationing meat, cheese, and butter.

MARCH 30

1964 Art Fleming hosts the first-ever episode of *Jeopardy!*

1867 Russia sells Alaska to the U.S. for $7.2 million.

JAN
FEB
MAR
APR
MAY
JUN
JUL
AUG
SEP
OCT
NOV
DEC

2001 Michael Phelps, at just fifteen years old, smashes the world record for the 200-meter butterfly.

1858 The first pencil with an attached eraser receives a patent.

1998 BMW purchases Rolls-Royce for $570 million.

1853 Famous Impressionist painter Vincent van Gogh is born in the Netherlands.

1981 An assassination attempt is made on President Ronald Reagan in Washington, D.C.

MARCH 31

1971 Starbucks Coffeehouse Company begins in Seattle, Washington.

1923 New York City hosts the first dance marathon.

1889 The Eiffel Tower officially opens in Paris.

2016 Apple releases its newest phone, the iPhone SE.

1909 Construction begins on the *Titanic*.

1940 New York officially opens the LaGuardia airport.

1984 *Lifestyles of the Rich and Famous* with host Robin Leach debuts on television.

2002 Tennis great Andre Agassi wins his 700th career match over Roger Federer.

 ## APRIL 1

2007 The first *Diary of a Wimpy Kid* book releases.

2020 Shenzhen becomes the first Chinese city to ban the eating of cats and dogs.

2004 Google begins its free email service, Gmail.

1970 President Richard Nixon bans television and radio advertisements of cigarettes.

Former president Richard Nixon in 1990

1778 The dollar sign has its beginning, thanks to Oliver Pollock.

1929 Louie Marx introduces the yo-yo in the U.S.

1891 William Wrigley, Jr. founds the Wrigley Company (famous for chewing gum).

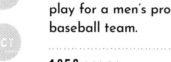

APRIL 2

1917 Jeannette Pickering becomes the first woman to serve in the US House of Representatives.

1931 Virne "Jackie" Mitchell becomes the first female to play for a men's pro baseball team.

1958 NASA becomes the official replacement name for the National Advisory Council on Aeronautics.

1939 American Motown singer Marvin Gaye is born in Washington, D.C.

1877 The White House hosts the first egg roll on the south lawn.

1877 Fourteen-year-old Rossa Matilda Ritcher becomes

The White House egg roll in 1990.

 JAN

 FEB

 MAR

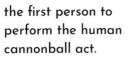 APR

the first person to perform the human cannonball act.

1513 Explorer Juan Ponce de León claims Florida for Spain.

1866 Except for Texas, President Andrew Johnson declares the end of the Civil War.

 MAY

 JUN

 JUL

 APRIL 3

 AUG

SEP

OCT

NOV

DEC

1973 General Manager of Motorola makes the first portable cell phone call.

1860 The Pony Express mail service begins with a route

from Missouri to California.

1961 Actor and comedian Eddie Murphy is born in Brooklyn, New York.

1892 Pharmacy owner Chester Platt and pastor John Scott invent the ice cream sundae in Ithaca, New York.

2011 Actress Penelope Cruz receives her star on the Hollywood Walk of Fame.

1910 Mt. McKinley, the tallest mountain in North America, is climbed for the first time by four local men.

1933 An airplane flies over Mt. Everest for the first time.

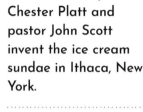

APRIL 4

1974 Hank Aaron ties Babe Ruth's record for 714 home runs.

1973 The World Trade Center is dedicated in New York City.

1968 Martin Luther King Jr. dies by assassination in Memphis, Tennessee.

1887 In Argonia, Kansas, Susanna Salter becomes America's first female elected mayor.

1949 Twelve nations sign the North Atlantic Treaty, giving NATO its start.

1996 Jaguar unveils its new SK8 convertible at the International Auto Show in New York.

1969 Surgeon Denton Cooley becomes the first doctor to implant an artificial heart in a human.

1850 Los Angeles officially becomes a city with a population of 1,600.

APRIL 5

1614 Native American Pocahontas marries Englishman Captain John Rolfe.

1792 The first veto in US history occurs when President Washington vetoes the Apportionment Bill.

2021 Colin Powell, US statesman and general, dies in Maryland at age eighty-four.

1621 The *Mayflower* leaves the Plymouth colony in Massachusetts to return to England.

1722 Explorer Jacob Roggeveen discovers Easter Island.

1887 Helen Keller learns the sign for "water" from

JAN
FEB
MAR
APR
MAY
JUN
JUL
AUG
SEP
OCT
NOV
DEC

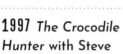

The Moais of Ahu Tongariki on Easter Island

her teacher, Anne Sullivan.

1997 *The Crocodile Hunter* with Steve Irwin debuts

2021 Baylor becomes the 82nd NCAA Basketball Champions with their defeat of Gonzaga.

APRIL 6

1483 Italian architect and painter, Raphael, is born in Urbino, Italy.

2009 The Basketball Hall of Fame inducts all-star Michael Jordan.

1980 3M begins the sale of Post-It Notes in the U.S.

1917 The U.S. enters World War I by declaring war on Germany.

Joseph Smith, founder of the Church of Jesus Christ of Latter-day Saints

1830 Joseph Smith organizes the Church of Jesus Christ of Latter-day Saints in Fayette, New York.

1930 James Dewar invents the Twinkie.

1909 Robert Peary becomes the first explorer to reach the North Pole.

1938 DuPont accidentally discovers Teflon.

 ## APRIL 7

1947 Ford Motor Company founder, Henry Ford, dies at age eighty-three.

1963 American pro golfer Jack Nicklaus wins his first Masters Tournament at age twenty-three.

1968 Rioting occurs in over one hundred US cities following the assassination of Martin Luther King Jr.

2021 A new record is set for the most expensive comic book ever, with a sale price of $3.25 million.

1827 Matches are sold for the first time.

2006 At least eleven tornadoes touch down in ten Tennessee counties.

APRIL 8

1986 Actor Clint Eastwood is elected as mayor of Carmel, California.

2011 Construction begins on the new Disneyland in Shanghai, China.

1989 Jim Abbott makes his MLB debut as a pitcher born with only one hand.

1994 Smoking is banned on US military bases and in the Pentagon.

1904 Times Square becomes the new name for Long Acre Square in Manhattan, New York.

1879 Milk is sold in glass bottles for the first time.

1879 J.R. Winters receives a patent for his fire escape ladder.

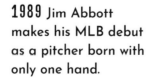

1974 Cubism pioneer Pablo Picasso dies in France at age ninety-one.

 # APRIL 9

1970 Paul McCartney announces the end of the Beatles.

1965 The Houston Astrodome stadium officially opens.

1865 The Civil War effectively ends with General Robert E. Lee signing a treaty of surrender.

1959 The Mercury Seven, NASA's first astronauts, are selected.

1912 The first baseball game at Fenway Park is played.

2012 *The Lion King* surpasses *The Phantom of the Opera* as the highest-grossing Broadway show.

1913 Ebbets Field, home of the Brooklyn Dodgers, opens for the first time.

2003 Baghdad falls to US-led forces in the Iraq War.

APRIL 10

2019 The first image of a black hole is released.

1849 US inventor Walter Hunt patents the safety pin.

1925 F. Scott Fitzgerald publishes *The Great Gatsby*.

2019 First-ever home delivery service by drone begins in Australia.

1912 The *Titanic* sets sail from Southampton, England.

1936 NFL coaching legend John Madden is born in Austin, Minnesota.

1633 Bananas go on sale for the first time in London.

1825 Hawaii opens its first hotel.

 # APRIL 11

1970: *Apollo 13* launches from Cape Canaveral, Florida.

1962 Newly established New York Mets play their first game.

The Apollo 13 LEM capsule

JAN
FEB
MAR
APR
MAY
JUN
JUL
AUG
SEP
OCT
NOV
DEC

1948 A general press release announces the discovery of the Dead Sea Scrolls.

1968 The Civil Rights Act is signed by President Lyndon B. Johnson.

2012 Marvel's *The Avengers* premieres in Los Angeles.

1895 Anaheim, California, installs its new electric light system.

1996 The Detroit Red Wings wins sixty season games, only the second NHL team to do so.

 ## APRIL 12

1981 NASA launches the first reusable space shuttle, *Columbia*.

1861 The American Civil War begins at Fort Sumter, South Carolina.

1877 A catcher's mask is used for the first time in a baseball game.

1954 Bill Haley and His Comets release *Rock Around the Clock*.

1992 Disneyland Paris opens in Marne-La-Vallee, France.

2012 The Candy Crush Saga video game releases on Facebook.

1853 New York puts the first truancy law into effect, which fines parents if their children miss school.

 # APRIL 13

1976 The new $2 bill is put into circulation in the U.S.

1743 Thomas Jefferson is born in Shadwell, Virginia.

1997 Tiger Woods becomes the youngest golfer to win the Masters Tournament at age twenty-one.

2013 Beijing, China, reports its first case of the H7N9 bird flu.

1943 The Thomas Jefferson Memorial

is dedicated in Washington, D.C.

1998 Dolly, the world's first cloned sheep, gives birth to a baby lamb.

1979 The world's longest table tennis match lasts over 101 hours in Sacramento, California.

1860 The first letter through the Pony Express reaches Sacramento, California.

An 1861 illustration of the Pony Express

APRIL 14

1954 Ford Motors debuts the Ford Mustang.

1865 President Abraham Lincoln is shot while attending Ford's Theater in Washington, D.C.

1939 *The Grapes of Wrath*, a novel by John Steinbeck, is published.

JAN

FEB

MAR

APR
MAY
JUN
JUL
AUG
SEP
OCT
NOV

DEC

JAN

FEB

MAR

APR

MAY

JUN

JUL

AUG

SEP

OCT

NOV

DEC

1912 The "unsinkable" *Titanic* strikes an iceberg off Newfoundland.

1901 James Cash Penney (J.C. Penney) opens his first store in Kemmerer, Wyoming.

1935 Severe dust storms hit the US Midwest on what would come to be called "Black Sunday."

1866 Anne Sullivan, the renowned teacher of Helen Keller, is born near Springfield, Massachusetts.

📑 APRIL 15

1452 Artist and scientist Leonardo da Vinci is born in Vinci, Italy.

1912 The *Titanic* officially sinks at 2:27 am while en route to New York City.

Replica of the first McDonald's in Des Plaines, Illinois

1955 The first McDonald's franchise opens in Des Plaines, Illinois.

1770 Joseph Priestly, an English chemist, discovers the rubber eraser.

1947 Jackie Robinson breaks the color barrier by becoming the first African American MLB player.

1817 America's first school for the deaf opens in Hartford, Connecticut.

1923 Insulin for diabetics becomes generally available.

1983 A new Tokyo Disneyland opens in Urayasu, Japan.

 # APRIL 16

1917 The first James Bond actor, Barry Nelson, is born in San Francisco.

1908 The Natural Bridges National Monument is established in southeastern Utah.

1962 Walter Cronkite, later known as "the most trusted man in America," becomes the anchor of *CBS Evening News*.

 JAN
 FEB
 MAR
 APR
 MAY
 JUN
JUL
AUG
SEP
OCT
NOV
DEC

1912 Harriet Quimby, an American aviator, becomes the first woman to fly across the English Channel.

1972 NASA launches *Apollo 16* from Cape Canaveral, Florida.

2007 Walmart reaches the number one spot on the Fortune 500 business list.

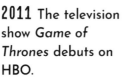

APRIL 17

1937 Cartoon character Daffy Duck first makes his first appearance.

2011 The television show *Game of Thrones* debuts on HBO.

1951 Mickey Mantle makes his MLB debut playing for the New York Yankees.

1861 The state of Virginia secedes from the Union during the Civil War.

1964 The Ford Mustang goes on sale with a starting price of $2,368.

1968 The Oakland A's play their first game in the Oakland-Alameda Stadium.

1983 MLB pitching legend Nolan Ryan strikes out his 3,500th batter.

2017 The world's first living giant shipworm is found in the Philippines.

 # APRIL 18

1906 San Francisco feels one of its most powerful earthquakes ever recorded with a 7.9 magnitude on the Richter scale.

1923 New York Yankees play in their stadium for the first time.

1924 The first crossword puzzle book is published by Simon and Schuster.

1775 Paul Revere makes his famous ride to warn Boston of the impending British attack.

Silversmith Paul Revere

JAN
FEB
MAR
APR
MAY
JUN
JUL
AUG
SEP
OCT
NOV
DEC

2012 Longtime television personality Dick Clark dies at age eighty-two.

....

1935 The first laundromat, "Wash-a-teria", opens in Fort Worth, Texas.

....

1995 Joe Montana retires from the NFL after eleven seasons.

....

1949 Ireland becomes its own republic, while Northern Ireland remains part of the United Kingdom.

....

 ## APRIL 19

1897 The first Boston Marathon is won by John J. McDermott.

....

1928 The Oxford English Dictionary

is published in its entirety—ten volumes!

....

1775 The American Revolution officially begins with the "shot

An illustration depicting the Battle of Lexington and Concord, or, "the shot heard round the world."

heard round the world."

2016 Daljinder Kaur, aged seventy-two, becomes the oldest woman on record to give birth.

1882 English naturalist Charles Darwin dies at age seventy-three.

1973 Pepsi becomes the first consumer product sole in the Soviet Union.

1982 Sally Ride becomes the first woman astronaut.

1995 The Oklahoma City bombing becomes one of the largest domestic terrorist attacks in the U.S.

 # APRIL 20

2010 The Deepwater Oil spill, the largest in history, occurs in the Gulf of Mexico.

1959 Country music star Dolly Parton releases her first single, *Puppy Love*, at age thirteen.

1940 The first public demonstration is given of the electron microscope.

 JAN
 FEB
 MAR
APR
 MAY
 JUN
 JUL
AUG
SEP
OCT
NOV
DEC

2020 For the first time in history, the price of US oil turns negative with falling worldwide demand.

....

1836 The US Congress creates the territory of Wisconsin.

....

1988 US Air force unveils the stealth (B-2) bomber.

....

1999 Actress Jane Seymour receives her star on the Hollywood Walk of Fame.

....

2016 US Treasury Department announces that Harriet Tubman will replace Andrew Jackson on the $20 bill.

....

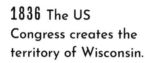

APRIL 21

1962 The Eye of the Needle, the first revolving restaurant in the U.S., opens in Seattle, Washington.

....

1876 New York City installs the nation's first flagpole.

....

1926 Queen Elizabeth II is born in Mayfair, London.

....

1977 The popular musical *Annie* opens for the first time on Broadway.

....

1789 John Adams is sworn in as the first

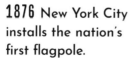

*The 1989
Game Boy*

vice president of the United States.

1898 Spain declares war on the U.S., starting the Spanish-American War.

1993 Chuck Norris first stars in the new action television series *Walker, Texas Ranger*.

1989 Nintendo releases the Game Boy in Japan.

 # APRIL 22

1970 US senator Gaylord Nelson founds Earth Day.

1952 The first US coast-to-coast nationally televised atomic bomb explosion.

2016 Over 170 countries sign the Paris Agreement, a pact to fight climate change.

 JAN
 FEB
MAR
APR
 MAY
JUN
JUL
 AUG
 SEP
OCT
 NOV
 DEC

1976 Barbara Walters becomes the first woman to co-anchor a nightly network news program.

....

1945 Sachsenhausen concentration camp, located near Berlin, Germany, is liberated.

....

1998 Disney's Animal Kingdom opens in Orlando, Florida.

....

2019 Marvel's *Avengers: Endgame* premieres in Los Angeles.

....

 **APRIL 23**

1616 William Shakespeare dies in Stratford-upon-Avon, England.

....

1914 Wrigley Field opens for its first MLB game.

....

1635 Boston Latin School, the

An illustration of William Shakespeare

first American public school, opens in Boston, Massachusetts.

2009 Singer and musician Taylor Swift begins her "Fearless" tour.

1985 Coca-Cola announces changes to its soda formula (they shortly returned to the original formula).

2009 iTunes reaches its 1 billionth download milestone.

2005 YouTube has its first video upload.

1968 The United Methodist Church is founded in Dallas, Texas.

 # APRIL 24

1990 NASA launches the Hubble Space Telescope, named after astronomer Edwin Hubble.

1888 George Eastman founds the Eastman Kodak Company.

1897 William Price becomes the first White House reporter.

1991 Garth Brooks and Reba McEntire win the 26th Academy of Country Music Awards.

 JAN
 FEB
 MAR
 APR
 MAY
JUN
JUL
AUG
SEP
OCT
NOV
DEC

2004 Eli Manning is the number one draft pick to the San Diego Chargers.

....

1942 American singer, actress, and Oscar winner Barbra Streisand is born in Brooklyn, New York.

....

2005 Joseph Ratzinger becomes Pope Benedict XVI in Vatican City.

....

📑 APRIL 25

1947 The White House opens its two-lane bowling alley.

....

1901 New York requires license plates on automobiles and motorcycles.

....

1954 Bell Labs announces its invention of the first solar battery made from silicon.

....

1960 The USS submarine *Triton* completes the first submerged circumnavigation of the earth.

....

1994 Southern California receives a shocking fourteen inches of snow.

....

2019 Just behind Apple and Amazon, Microsoft becomes the third US firm to have a market worth of $1 trillion.

hits his 250th home run.

1997 Ken Griffey Jr. of the Seattle Mariners

1993 Boris Yeltsin is elected as President of Russia.

APRIL 26

1989 Comedian and actress Lucille Ball dies at age seventy-seven in Los Angeles.

2011 The singing competition reality show, *The Voice*, premieres on NBC.

1954 Mass trials of the polio vaccine begin.

1933 Nazi Germany establishes its secret police force, the Gestapo.

Lucille Ball in the late 1980s

JAN FEB MAR APR MAY JUN JUL AUG SEP OCT NOV DEC

1803 Thousands of meteor fragments fall in L'Aigle, France, after a meteorite shower.

1912 Hugh Bradley of the Red Sox hits the first home run in Fenway Park.

1976 Non-stop flights begin on Pan Am from New York City to Tokyo.

📑 APRIL 27

1931 Hawaii records its hottest day ever at 100°F.

1810 Beethoven composes *Fur Elise*, one of the world's most famous piano pieces.

1773 Britain imposes the Tea Act on American colonists.

Coretta Scott King with President Ronald Reagan in 1983

1927 Coretta Scott King, civil rights activist and wife of Martin Luther King Jr., is born in Alabama.

1981 Xerox premiers the first personal computer mouse.

2021 Pfizer announces its work on a new antiviral therapy to help treat COVID-19.

1991 David Ozio wins the Firestone World Bowling Tournament of Champions in Ohio.

 # APRIL 28

1926 Author Harper Lee, known for her novel *To Kill a Mockingbird*, is born in Monroeville, Alabama.

2001 Dennis Tito spends $20 million to become the first space tourist.

1994 The 100th episode of *The Simpsons* airs on Fox TV.

1788 Maryland becomes the seventh state to join the Union.

2004 Shrek the sheep is shorn on live TV, its fleece weighing 60 pounds!

APR

2000 Talk show host and comedian Jay Leno receive his star on the Hollywood Walk of Fame.

2008 Scientists dissect a rare colossal squid for research in New Zealand.

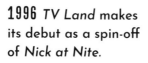

APRIL 29

2011 Prince William and Kate Middleton wed at Westminster Abbey in London.

1945 US Seventh Army liberates Dachau, the Nazi concentration camp.

2019 Due to the city sinking, Indonesia announces plans to move the capital from Jakarta.

2004 After 107 years in production, the last Oldsmobile is manufactured.

1996 *TV Land* makes its debut as a spin-off of *Nick at Nite*.

2019 700 cases of measles are reported in the U.S., the highest number in twenty-five years.

1967 Aretha Franklin wins Billboard's Song of the Year with *Respect*.

1863 American newspaper publisher William Randolph

Hearst is born in San
Francisco.

....

📑 **APRIL 30**

*A Mr. Potato
Head parade
balloon in
2015*

1789 George
Washington is
officially inaugurated
as the first US
president.

....

1812 Louisiana joins
the Union as the
eighteenth state.

....

1900 Hawaii becomes
an official US
territory.

....

1952 Mr. Potato Head
becomes the first
toy to be marketed
to children by a
television commercial.

....

1905 Albert Einstein
completes his Ph.D.
at the University of
Zurich.

....

1864 New York
becomes the first

JAN FEB MAR APR MAY JUN JUL AUG SEP OCT NOV DEC

JAN

FEB

MAR

APR

MAY

JUN

JUL

AUG

SEP
OCT

NOV
DEC

state to charge a fee for a hunting license.

2015 Jameis Winston of Florida State becomes the first draft pick for the Tampa Bay Buccaneers.

2018 The oldest living spider in the world, a female trapdoor, dies at age forty-three.

MAY 1

1999 *SpongeBob SquarePants* debuts on Nickelodeon.

1963 Mountaineer Jim Whittaker becomes the first American to reach the summit of Mt. Everest.

1941 General Mills introduces Cheerios.

1971 Amtrak passenger trains begin service.

1930 Eleven-year-old Venetia Burney officially names Pluto.

An Amtrak passenger train.

1930 New York City opens the Empire State Building.

1991 Oakland A's Rickey Henderson steals his 939th base in the MLB.

MAY 2

1803 France sells the Louisiana Territory to the U.S. for $15 million.

1611 The King James Version of the Bible is first published.

2000 President Bill Clinton announces GPS availability for public use.

1878 The US Mint ceases production of the 20-cent coin.

1908 Composer Albert von Tilzer and lyricist Jack Norworth copyright the tune *Take Me Out to the Ball Game.*

1974 Thriller film *Jaws* begins filming in Marth's Vineyard, Massachusets.

1885 The first issue of *Good Housekeeping* magazine is published.

2011 American armed forces kill terrorist Osama bin Laden in Pakistan.

JAN
FEB
MAR
APR
MAY
JUN
JUL
AUG
SEP
OCT
NOV
DEC

MAY 3

1802 Washington D.C. officially becomes a city.

1948 *CBS Evening New* airs its first broadcast.

1937 Author Margaret Mitchell wins the Pulitzer Prize for her novel *Gone with the Wind*.

1494 Christopher Columbus discovers the island of Jamaica (naming it St. Jago).

1921 The first state sales tax takes effect in West Virginia.

2000 The first cache is placed in the sport of geocaching.

MAY 4

1929 Actress Audrey Hepburn is born in Brussels, Belgium.

1904 Construction begins on the Panama Canal.

2021 Halima Cisse of Malia becomes the third woman to give birth to nonuplets (nine babies).

2018 California surpasses Great

Prime Minister Margaret Thatcher in 1991

Britain as the world's fifth-largest economy.

1878 Thomas Edison demonstrates his phonograph for the first time at the Grand Opera House.

1979 Britain elects its first female prime minister, Margaret Thatcher.

2002 Barry Bonds, of the San Francisco Giants, hits his 400th home run.

MAY 5

1988 English songwriter and singer Adele is born in London.

1921 Gabrielle "Coco" Chanel releases her first perfume, Chanel No. 5.

1961 Alan Shepard Jr. becomes the first US astronaut in space.

 JAN
 FEB
 MAR
 APR
 MAY
 JUN
 JUL
 AUG
 SEP
 OCT
NOV
DEC

MAY

1813 Mary Kries become the first US woman to receive a patent, which was for her technique for weaving straw with silk.

....

1862 Mexico defeats French forces and Cinco de Mayo is born!

....

1818 German philosopher Karl Marx is born in Trier, Germany.

....

1968 McDonald's debuts the Big Mac.

....

2021 Canada is the first country to authorize COVID-19 vaccines for youth aged twelve to fifteen.

....

MAY 6

1954 Roger Bannister becomes the first person to run a mile in under four minutes.

2019 The United Nations reports that one million plant and animal species are at

Elon Musk in 2015.

risk of extinction if action is not taken.

2002 Elon Musk launches SpaceX.

1997 The Bee Gees and Michael Jackson are inducted into the Rock and Roll Hall of Fame.

1957 The final episode of *I Love Lucy*, starring Lucille Ball, airs on television.

1856 Austrian psychoanalyst Sigmund Freud is born in Příbor, Czechoslovakia.

 ## MAY 7

1838 Jenny Lind, "The Swedish Nightingale," makes her opera debut.

1876 Alexander Graham bell receives the patent for the telephone.

1979 NASA's *Voyager I* reaches Jupiter.

2005 Mike Smith wins the 131st Kentucky Derby aboard Giacomo.

1975 President Ford declares an end to the Vietnam era.

1789 New York City hosts the first US Presidential Inaugural Ball.

JAN FEB MAR APR MAY JUN JUL AUG SEP OCT NOV DEC

MAY 8

1980 The World Health Assembly certifies that smallpox is eradicated.

1945 World War II in Europe officially ends.

1348 The Black Death begins in England.

1792 The US Congress establishes the military draft.

1959 Mike and Marian Ilitch found Little Caesars Pizza in Garden City, Michigan.

1954 Parry O'Brien sets a record for the farthest shot-put throw to date at 60 feet and 5.25 inches.

 # MAY 9

1502 Christopher Columbus sets sail on his final voyage in hopes of finding a passage to Asia.

1950 Smokey Bear becomes the national symbol for wildfire prevention.

1712 North and South Carolina

are born from the dividing the Carolina Territory.

....

1994 South Africa chooses Nelson Mandela as its first Black president.

....

1868 Reno, Nevada, becomes a city.

....

2018 French adventurer Jean-Jacques Savin successfully crosses the Atlantic Ocean in a barrel-shaped capsule.

....

 # MAY 10

1503 Christopher Columbus sights the Cayman Islands.

....

1869 The US transcontinental railroad is completed at Promontory Point, Utah.

....

1508 Italian artist Michaelangelo starts his work on the Sistine Chapel.

....

Artist Michaelangelo

JAN
FEB
MAR
APR
MAY
JUN
JUL
AUG
SEP
OCT
NOV
DEC

1962 The first issue of Marvel's *The Incredible Hulk* comic book debuts.

....

1818 Paul Revere, dies in Boston, Massachusetts.

....

2002 Dr. Pepper announces a new

flavor for the first time in 117 years: Red Fusion.

....

2001 Boeing announces it's changing the location of its headquarters from Seattle to Chicago.

....

 **MAY 11**

1858 Minnesota becomes the thirty-second state to join the Union.

....

1947 B. R. Goodrich Company announces its new tubeless tire.

....

A crowd celebrates at a Republic Day Parade in India

2000 The population of India officially reaches one billion.

2021 The Chinese census shows its slowest population growth since the 1960s.

1910 Glacier National Park is formed in Montana.

1987 John Hopkins surgeons perform the first heart-lung transplant.

1969 Monty Python, the British comedy troupe, forms.

MAY 12

1930 The Adler Planetarium in Chicago is the first of its kind to open to the public in the Western hemisphere.

1846 The Donner Party departs for California from Independence, Missouri.

1960 Elvis Presley is the special guest on a Frank Sinatra television special.

2017 Harry Styles releases his solo album *Harry Styles*.

2008 The price for first-class US stamps

rises from 41 cents to 42 cents.

1965 International Nurses Day is founded in memory of Florence Nightingale.

1979 Tennis great Chris Evert ends her 125-match winning streak.

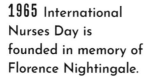 **MAY 13**

1970 The Beatles film *Let it Be* premieres worldwide in New York City.

1950 American music legend Stevie Wonder is born in Saginaw, Michigan.

1958 Velcro registers for a trademark.

1975 Tennis-ball-sized hail hits Wernersville, Tennessee.

1940 Winston Churchill makes his first speech to the House of Commons as prime minister of Britain.

1967 Octagon-shaped boxing rings are tested in hopes of fewer corner injuries.

1982 The Chicago Cubs beat the Astros to win their 800th game.

2019 Hollywood star Doris Day dies at age ninety-three.

MAY 14

1856 The first camels in the U.S. arrive from Turkey.

1804 Famous explorers Lewis and Clark begin their exploration of the Louisiana Purchase.

1944 George Lucas, the creator of *Star Wars,* is born in Modesto, California.

1998 Television comedy show *Seinfeld* airs its last episode.

1984 Mark Zuckerberg, the co-founder of Facebook, is born in White Plains, New York.

Mark Zuckerberg in 2018

JAN
FEB
MAR
APR
MAY
JUN
JUL
AUG
SEP
OCT
NOV
DEC

1607 Jamestown, Virginia, becomes North America's first permanent English settlement.

2016 Surfer Gabriel Medina becomes the first to land the backflip move in a competition.

📑 MARY 15

1940 Women's nylon stockings hit the market, selling out in just four days.

1928 The first cartoon featuring Mickey Mouse is screen-tested as a silent film.

1922 Amelia Earhart receives her pilot's license.

1951 AT&T becomes the first US corporation with one million stockholders.

1990 Vincent van Gogh's *Portrait*

"Portrait of Doctor Gachet" by Vincent van Gogh

of *Doctor Gachet* painting sells for a record-breaking $82.5 million

....

2010 Jessica Watson, at age sixteen, becomes the youngest person to attempt to sail a solo, unassisted, non-stop trip around the world.

....

 ## MAY 16

1986 *Top Gun*, starring Tom Cruise, is released in American theaters.

....

1975 Junko Tabei becomes the first woman to reach the summit of Mt. Everest.

....

1866 The US Congress authorizes the nickel, replacing the silver half-dime.

....

2013 Bill Gates regains his title of "World's Richest Man" after losing it in 2008.

....

1939 The first US food stamps are issued in Rochester, New York.

....

2000 Hilary Clinton becomes the first former US First Lady to run for public office.

....

 JAN
 FEB
 MAR
 APR
 MAY
JUN
JUL
 AUG
 SEP
 OCT
NOV
DEC

MAY 17

1792 The New York Stock Exchange begins at 70 Wall Street in New York City.

· ·

1875 Louisville, Kentucky, hosts the first Kentucky Derby horse race.

· ·

1939 The first televised fashion show airs from the Ritz-Carlton Hotel in New York.

· ·

2002 Legoland opens in Gunzburg, Germany.

· ·

1954 The US Supreme Court bans segregation in schools.

· ·

2009 A beta version of Minecraft is released for testing.

· ·

2020 An autographed pair of Michael Jordan's Air Nike 1s sells for $560,000 at auction.

· ·

MAY 18

1980 Mount St. Helens erupts three times in twenty-four hours.

· ·

1953 Jacqueline Cochran becomes the first woman to break the sound barrier

Steam rises from Mount St. Helens in 1980 sometime of its erruption

(which requires flying faster than 770 miles per hour if at sea level).

. . . .

2012 Facebook begins trading on the NASDAQ.

. . . .

1860 Abraham Lincoln becomes the Republican Party nominee for president.

. . . .

2001 At 101 years old, Harold Stilson becomes the oldest golfer to record a hole-in-one.

. . . .

2001 DreamWorks Pictures releases the movie *Shrek*.

. . . .

2018 BTS, a K-pop boy band, releases the album *Love Yourself: Tear*.

. . . .

2004 At age forty, Randy Johnson becomes the oldest MLB pitcher to throw a perfect game.

. . . .

MAY 19

JAN

 FEB

 MAR

 APR

MAY

 JUN

 JUL

 AUG

SEP

OCT

NOV

 DEC

1946 Actor and wrestler Andre the Giant is born in Coulommiers, France.

2018 Britain's Prince Harry marries Meghan Markle at Windsor Castle.

1884 Ringling Brothers opens its first circus show in Baraboo, Wisconsin.

1995 The world's youngest doctor, Balamurali Ambati, graduates from medical school at age seventeen.

2020 A study announces a seventeen percent drop in greenhouse gas emissions worldwide (for April) as a result of COVID-19 lockdowns.

 **MAY 20**

Illustration of Charles Lindbergh and his plane, the "Spirit of St. Louis"

1927 Charles Lindbergh makes the first solo transatlantic flight from New York to Paris.

1992 Chicago bans the selling of spray paint in hopes of reducing graffiti.

1908 Oscar-winning actor James Stewart is born in Indiana, Pennsylvania.

1862 President Lincoln signs the Homestead Act, providing 160 acres of land for free to those who will live on it and cultivate it for at least five years.

1506 Italian explorer Christopher Columbus dies in Valladolid, Spain.

1983 Billboard Song of the Year goes to *Every Breath You Take* by The Police.

1979 Britain's Elton John becomes the first Western pop star to tour the USSR.

 MAY 21

1881 Clara Burton founds the American Red Cross.

1738 John and Charles Wesley found the Methodist Church.

1941 The *S.S. Robin Moor*, the first American ship to sink in World War II, is attacked by a German U-boat. No lives are lost.

1914 The Greyhound Bus Company begins in Minnesota.

1934 Oskaloosa, Iowa, becomes the first US city to fingerprint all of its citizens.

1980 George Lucas's *Star Wars: Empire Strikes Back* opens in theaters.

2013 Microsoft announces an upcoming release of the Xbox One.

 # MAY 22

1992 Comedian Johnny Carson makes his final appearance as host of *The Tonight Show*.

1972 President Nixon becomes the first US president to visit the Soviet Union.

2011 The U.S. experiences one of its worst tornadoes in Joplin, Missouri.

1803 Connecticut becomes the first state to open a public library.

Dwayne Johnson in 2019

JAN
FEB
MAR
APR
MAY
JUN
JUL
AUG
SEP
OCT
NOV
DEC

1931 Canned rattlesnake meat goes on sale in Florida.

2018 Stacey Cunningham becomes the first woman to head the New York Stock Exchange.

2015 Actor Dwayne Johnson sets a record for the most selfies taken in three minutes (105 of them).

 ## MAY 23

1962 Doctors in Boston perform the first successful reattachment of a human limb.

1984 Lucasfilm releases the movie *Indiana Jones and the Temple of Doom.*

1785 Benjamin Franklin announces his invention of bifocal eyeglasses.

1788 South Carolina becomes the eighth state to join the Union.

1900 William Carney, a Civil War hero, becomes the first African American to receive the Medal of Honor.

2000 Rap artist Eminem's album *The Marshall Mathers LP* becomes the fastest-selling rap album in history.

1903 The first automobile road trip across the U.S. leaves San Francisco for New York.

1946 The first Chick-fil-A restaurant opens in Georgia.

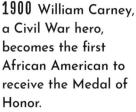 **MAY 24**

1887 The Brooklyn Bridge officially opens, connecting New York City and Brooklyn.

Bob Dylan receives the Presidential Medal of Freedom in 2012

1941 Singer-songwriter Bob Dylan is born in Duluth, Minnesota.

1938 The first coin-controlled parking meter gets a patent.

1844 The first telegraph message is sent by Samuel Morse.

2001 Sherpa Temba Tsheri becomes the youngest person to climb to the top of Mt. Everest at age fifteen.

2004 The country of North Korea bans cell phones.

2020 The front page of the *New York Times* lists almost 1,000 people who had died from COVID-19.

 ## MAY 25

1977 *Star Wars: A New Hope* is released and becomes an overnight sensation.

1935 Jesse Owens sets world records for the broad jump, the 220-yard dash, and the 220-yard low hurdles.

1935 Baseball great Babe Ruth hits his last home run (number 714!).

 JAN
 FEB
MAR
 APR
MAY
 JUN
JUL
AUG
SEP
OCT
NOV
DEC

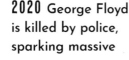

1961 President John F. Kennedy announces his commitment to have a man on the moon by the end of the decade.

2011 *The Oprah Winfrey Show* airs its last episode.

2020 George Floyd is killed by police, sparking massive protests around the U.S.

1787 Philadelphia hosts the US Constitutional Convention.

2012 The first commercial spacecraft, SpaceX's Dragon, lands at the International Space Station.

 **MAY 26**

1994 Michael Jackson and Lisa Marie Presley marry in the Dominican Republic.

1927 Ford Motors manufactures its last Model T motor car.

1993 Carlos Martinez hits a ball off the head of Jose Canseco—for a home run!

1992 The first Dodge Viper rolls off the assembly line.

Sally Ride in 1986

1969 NASA's *Apollo 10* returns to earth.

2021 Amazon announces its intent to purchase the

Metro-Goldwyn-Mayer (MGM) television studio for $8.45 billion.

1951 Sally Ride is born in Encino, California.

MAY 27

1937 San Francisco's Golden Gate Bridge opens.

2016 Merriam-Webster's dictionary website classifies a hot dog as a sandwich.

1933 Disney releases the short film *Three Little Pigs*, which goes on to win an Academy Award.

1703 Russian Tsar Peter the Great

JAN
FEB
MAR
APR
MAY
JUN
JUL
AUG
SEP
OCT
NOV
DEC

founds Saint Petersburg.

1907 Breakouts of the Bubonic Plague hit San Francisco.

1969 Construction begins on Florida's Walt Disney World.

1995 Actor Christopher Reeves, best known for his role as Superman, becomes paralyzed after a horse accident.

MAY 28

2003 The first cloned horse, Prometea, is born to its genetic mother.

1952 Women in Greece are granted the right to vote.

1934 The first set of quintuplets (five

An illustration of Maya Angelou

babies) to survive infancy is born.

2014 Maya Angelou, the famous American poet, dies at age eighty-six.

1999 Leonardo de Vinci's *The Last Supper* painting is put back on display after twenty-two years of restoration work.

1892 John Muir founds the Sierra Club to help conserve nature.

1980 West Point Military Academy graduates its first class of women.

2018 The One World Trade Center officially opens the Observatory.

ᗰᗩY 29

1848 Wisconsin becomes the thirtieth state to join the Union.

1790 Rhode Island becomes the thirteenth state to join the Union.

1917 Future US president John F. Kennedy is born in Brookline, Massachusetts.

1942 Bing Crosby records *White Christmas*, making

one of the bestselling singles ever.

2004 President George W. Bush dedicates the World War II memorial in Washington, D.C.

2015 *Jurassic World* premieres in Paris.

1997 Rebecca Sealfon wins the 70th National Spelling Bee.

1984 The Boston Red Sox retire the jerseys of Ted Williams and Joe Cronin.

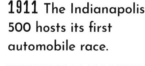 ## MAY 30

2003 Pixar's *Finding Nemo* is released in the U.S. and Canada.

1911 The Indianapolis 500 hosts its first automobile race.

1971 Blue Ribbon Sports changes its name to Nike, Inc.

1922 The Lincoln Memorial is dedicated in Washington, D.C.

1870 Following the Civil War, Texas is readmitted to the Union.

1971 NASA launches its first satellite to orbit Mars, the *Mariner 9*.

1964 *Love Me Do* by the Beatles hits number one on the music charts.

2020 Tesla's SpaceX's Crew Dragon-Demo 2 launches from the Kennedy Space Center.

 **MAY 31**

A vintage taxi cab

2014 Popular YouTube video *Gangnam Style* hits two billion views.

1935 Fox Film Corporation and 20th Century pictures merge to form 20th Century Fox.

1790 The U.S. enacts copyright law.

1907 Taxi cabs run for the first time in New York City.

1937 The first set of quadruplets graduate

 JAN
 FEB
 MAR
 APR
 MAY
 JUN
 JUL
 AUG
 SEP
 OCT
 NOV
 DEC

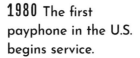

from college at Baylor University.

....

2004 The first episode of *Peppa Pig* airs on television.

....

📑 JUNE 1

1980 The first payphone in the U.S. begins service.

....

1792 Kentucky becomes the fifteenth state to join the Union.

....

2019 Warner Bros. announces Robert Pattinson will play the new Batman.

....

1796 Tennessee becomes the sixteenth state to join the Union.

....

2009 Due to the Great Recession, General Motors files for Chapter 11 bankruptcy.

....

An illustration of Helen Keller learning to communicate with teacher Anne Sullivan

1980 CNN becomes the first twenty-four-hour news channel.

1968 Hellen Keller dies in Westport, Connecticut, at age eighty-seven.

2017 The U.S. withdraws from the Paris Climate Agreement.

1997 The Children's Miracle Network Telethon raises $5,400,186 for children's hospitals.

 ## JUNE 2

1933 The White House opens its new swimming pool.

1953 Elizabeth II becomes Queen of England.

1851 Dole Food Company opens in Oahu, Hawaii.

1731 Martha Dandridge, the future wife of George Washington, is born in Virginia.

2004 *Jeopardy!* all-star Ken Jennings begins his seventy-four-game winning streak.

2017 *Wonder Woman* opens in theaters.

1896 Inventor Guglielmo Marconi applies for a patent for the radio.

2015 Volunteers in Bhutan set a world record for planting 49,672 trees in one hour.

  JUNE 3

1876 Britain and Canada are introduced to lacrosse.

1764 St. Louis, Missouri, becomes an official city.

1976 *Bohemian Rhapsody* by Queen sells over one million copies.

2012 Tiger Woods wins his seventy-third PGA tour.

2017 Museum dedicated to Dr. Seuss opens in Springfield, Massachusetts.

2019 *Forbes* magazine names Jay-Z the world's first billionaire rapper.

1959 The US Air Force Academy graduates its first class.

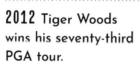 **JUNE 4**

Women working to encourage fellow women to vote in 1924

1942 The Battle of Midway begins between the U.S. and Japan.

1984 Bruce Springsteen releases *Born in the USA*.

1973 The ATM receives a patent.

1912 A national minimum wage is used for the first time in Massachusetts.

1892 The first Abercrombie & Fitch opens in Manhattan, New York.

1919 The US Senate approves the Nineteenth Amendment, which gives women the right to vote.

1940 Britain evacuates their 300,000 troops from Dunkirk.

1974 The Seattle Seahawks are granted a franchise by the NFL.

JAN
FEB
MAR
APR
MAY
JUN
JUN
JUL
AUG
SEP
OCT
NOV
DEC

JUNE 5

US President Ronald Reagan in 1984

 JUN

JUL

AUG

SEP

OCT

NOV

DEC

1917 The World War I army draft opens for men ages twenty-one to thirty.

1876 Americans are introduced to bananas at the World's Fair in Philadelphia.

1993 Ronald Reagan, the fortieth US president, dies at age ninety-three.

2018 The Miss America pageant declares an end to its swimsuit competition.

1998 Disney releases *Mulan.*

1964 The Rolling Stones begin their first concert tour in San Bernardino, California.

JUNE 6

1987 The New York Yankees play their 13,000th game.

1933 The first-ever drive-in movie theater opens in Pennsauken, New Jersey.

1882 H. W. Weely patents the electric iron.

1844 George Williams founds the YMCA in London.

1925 Auto manufacturer Chrysler begins.

1896 Frank Harbo and George Samuelson begin their attempt to cross the Atlantic in a rowboat (and they succeed!).

1984 Alexey Pajitnov creates the video game *Tetris*.

 # JUNE 7

1853 Japan begins trading with the West.

1981 The U.S. appoints its first female Supreme Court Justice, Sandra Day O'Connor.

JAN
 FEB
 MAR
 APR
 MAY
JUN
 JUL
 AUG
SEP
OCT
NOV
 DEC

1982 Graceland (home of Elvis Presley) opens for public tours in Memphis, Tennessee.

1912 A US airplane fires machine guns for the first time.

1959 Rock and Roll Hall of Fame legend Prince is born in Minneapolis, Minnesota.

2010 The Washington Nationals draft outfielder Bryce Harper as their number-one pick.

 # JUNE 8

1940 Edwin McMillan and Philip Abelson announce the discovery of neptunium.

1789 James Madison proposes the Bill of Rights to the US House of Representatives.

1925 The shortest-ever MLB player (under four feet), Eddie Gaedel, is born in Chicago, Illinois.

1889 Cable cars in Los Angeles begin service.

1917 Walt Disney graduates from Benton High School.

The firehouse used in the Ghostbusters film, today home to Hook & Ladder 8

1949 The country of Siam changes its name to Thailand.

1984 The comedy film *Ghostbusters* opens in theaters.

2013 Tennis star Serena Williams wins her second French Women's Open.

JUNE 9

2008 MLB player Ken Griffey Jr. hits his 600th career home run.

1973 The American racehorse, Secretariat, captures the Triple Crown.

1959 The *USS George Washington* becomes the first US ballistic-missile submarine to launch.

1784 The Catholic church organizes in

America under Father John Carroll.

. . . .

1958 Queen Elizabeth II opens the London Gatwick Airport.

. . . .

1870 English writer and Victorian novelist Charles Dickens dies at age fifty-eight.

. . . .

JUNE 10

1890 Wyoming becomes the forty-fourth state to join the Union.

. . . .

1847 The *Chicago Tribune* newspaper begins publication.

. . . .

1921 Prince Philip, the future husband of Queen Elizabeth II, is born in Greece.

. . . .

1922 Judy Garland, best known for playing Dorothy in *The Wizard of Oz*, is

An illustration of Judy Garland as Dorothy

born in Grand Rapids, Minnesota.

1963 President John F. Kennedy signs the Equal Pay Act into law.

1752 Benjamin Franklin flies a kite in a thunderstorm to demonstrate the connection between lightning and electricity.

2007 *I'm a Gummy Bear* novelty dance song debuts.

2018 Dust storm on Mars disrupts communication with NASA's *Opportunity Rover*.

 # JUNE 11

1929 Anne Frank is born in Frankfurt, Germany.

1982 Steven Spielberg's film *E.T.* opens in theaters.

1993 Steven Spielberg's film *Jurassic Park* opens in theaters.

1928 The U.S. receives its first seeing eye dog, Buddy, from Switzerland.

2002 *American Idol* debuts.

JUN

2010 The nineteenth World Cup soccer game is the first to be held on the African continent.

2009 The H1N1 Swine Flu becomes a global pandemic.

 **JUNE 12**

1942 Anne Frank receives her now-famous diary for her thirteenth birthday.

2016 Football star Cristiano Ronaldo makes *Forbes*'s Highest-Paid Athletes List at $88 million.

1924 Future US president George H.

W. Bush is born in Milton, Massachusetts.

1903 Niagara Falls, Ontario, becomes a city.

1997 A replica of Shakespeare's Globe Theater opens in London, England.

 **JUNE 13**

The real-life Green Gables home used in the Anne of Green Gables books

1920 The US postal service officially prohibits the mailing of children and animals.

1971 The *New York Times* begins publishing the "Pentagon Papers" (top-secret reports on US involvement in Vietnam).

1967 Thurgood Marshall becomes the first African American Supreme Court Justice.

1908 *Anne of Green Gables* is first published in Boston.

2021 Tennis great Novak Djokovic wins his nineteenth Grand Slam title.

1966 Miranda Rights go into effect ("You have the right to remain silent...").

1873 The first US policewoman, Alice Stebbins Wells, is born in Manhattan, Kansas.

 JAN

 FEB

 MAR

APR

MAY

 JUN

 JUL

 AUG

 SEP

 OCT

NOV

DEC

2000 Actor Samuel L. Jackson receives his star on the Hollywood Walk of Fame.

⌷ JUNE 14

1946 Donald Trump is born in New York, New York.

1954 "Under God" is added to the US Pledge of Allegiance.

1959 Disneyland opens its iconic monorail system.

1775 Congress establishes the United States Army.

1953 Elvis Prestley graduates from L.C. Humes High School in Memphis, Tennessee.

1940 The first prisoners arrive at the Auschwitz concentration camp.

Auschwitz concentration camp, today a memorial and museum

2009 Basketball coach Phil Jackson wins his tenth NBA championship.

1969 Tennis star Steffi Graf is born in Bruhl, Germany.

JUNE 15

1958 The first Pizza Hut restaurant opens in Wichita, Kansas.

1864 Arlington becomes the official US national cemetery.

1836 Arkansas becomes the twenty-fifth state to join the Union.

1215 King John of England signs the Magna Carta.

1846 Idaho, Oregon, and Washington all become US territories.

1667 Jean-Baptiste performs the first blood transfusion.

2007 Game show host Bob Barker steps down as host of *The Price is Right.*

1871 Phoebe Couzins becomes the first female to graduate from a US collegiate law school.

JUNE 16

1884 The first US roller coaster in America opens at Coney Island in Brooklyn, New York.

1893 F. W. Rueckheim introduces Cracker Jacks at the Chicago World's Fair.

1903 Henry Ford and associates found the Ford Motor Company.

1963 Valentina V. Tereshkova becomes the first woman in space.

2017 Amazon announces its purchase of Whole Foods for $13.7 billion.

2018 Beyonce and Jay-Z release their joint album, *Everything is Love.*

1938 American author Joyce Carol Oats is born in Lockport, New York.

 ## JUNE 17

1985 The Discovery Channel begins broadcasting.

1885 The Statue of Liberty, a gift from France, arrives in the U.S.

1871 Anna Swan and Martin Van Buren Bates become the

tallest-known couple in history to wed.

1870 George Cormack, the inventor of Wheaties cereal, is born in Minneapolis, Minnesota.

1992 Philadelphia 76ers trade power forward Charles Barkley to the Phoenix Suns.

1988 Microsoft Company releases MS-DOS 4.0.

1967 President Nixon declares that the US war on drugs has begun.

 # JUNE 18

1942 Paul McCartney is born in Liverpool, England.

1877 Inventor Thomas Edison records the human voice for the first time.

Paul McCartney in 2009

1812 The War of 1812 begins.

1990 Hale Irwin wins the first sudden-death US Open Golf Championship.

1873 Suffragette Susan B. Anthony receives a $100 fine for voting illegally.

1976 American singer Blake Shelton is born in Oklahoma.

2010 American rapper Eminem releases *Recovery*, his seventh album.

 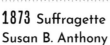

JUNE 19

1929 7-Up soda is introduced in the U.S.

1919 The U.S. celebrates Father's Day for the first time.

Cartoon featuring Garfield and Odie

1978 Jim Davis's comic strip *Garfield* debuts in forty newspapers.

1946 Joe Louis wins the first televised heavyweight boxing championship.

1903 Baseball Hall of Famer Lou Gehrig is born in Manhattan, New York.

2016 LeBron James leads the Cleveland Cavaliers to their first NBA title.

2015 Pixar's film *Inside Out* opens in theaters.

1992 *Batman Returns* starring Michael Keaton opens in theaters.

JUNE 20

1928 General Mills is founded in Minnesota.

1863 West Virginia becomes the thirty-fifth state to join the Union.

1960 Harry Belafonte becomes the first

African American to win an Emmy award.

1819 The SS *Savannah* become the first steamboat to cross the Atlantic Ocean.

JUN

2020 Verkhoyansk, Serbia records its highest ever temperature in the Arctic circle at 100°F.

....

 # JUNE 21

1961 Disney releases the comedy film *The Parent Trap*.

....

2003 J. K. Rowling publishes *Harry Potter and the Order of the Phoenix*.

....

1997 The WNBA plays its first game.

....

1982 Prince William of Wales is born to Prince Charles and Princess Diana.

....

1893 The first Ferris wheel makes its debut at the World's Columbian Exposition in Chicago.

....

1967 Douglas Engelbart files for a

A Frida Kahlo self-portrait

patent for the first computer mouse.

1834 Inventor Cyrus McCormick patents the reaping machine.

2001 Artist Frida Kahlo becomes the first Latina woman to be featured on a US postage stamp.

JUNE 22

1944 President Franklin Roosevelt signs the GI Bill of Rights (which provides benefits for war veterans).

1971 The U.S. lowers the voting age from twenty-one to eighteen through the Twenty-Sixth Amendment.

1955 Disney releases *Lady and the Tramp*.

1940 The first Dairy Queen opens in Joliet, Illinois.

1942 Congress formally adopts the Pledge of Allegiance.

1947 NBA standout "Pistol" Pete Maravich is born in Aliquippa, Pennsylvania.

2020 Japan's supercomputer, Fugaku, is declared the world's most powerful computer.

JUNE 23

1996 Nintendo launches the Nintendo 64.

2015 NASA's *Mars Odyssey* spacecraft completes its 60,000th orbit around Mars.

1860 US Congress forms the US Secret Service.

1846 Belgian instrument maker Adolphe Sax patents the saxophone.

1926 The first SAT (Scholastic Aptitude Test) exam is given to 8,000 students.

2016 The United Kingdom votes to leave the European Union (Brexit).

2018 Rameshbab Praggnanandhaa becomes the second-youngest chess grandmaster at age twelve.

Adolphe Sax as featured on a Belgian banknote

1980 *The David Letterman Show* debuts on NBC-TV.

 # JUNE 24

1994 Disney's *Lion King* opens in theaters and becomes the highest-grossing film of the year.

1987 Soccer star Lionel Messi is born in Argentina.

2010 The longest tennis match in history, lasting eleven hours and five minutes, is played between John Isner and Nicolas Mahut.

1916 Mary Pickford becomes the first female actress to be offered a contract of $1 million.

1901 Artist Pablo Picasso holds his first exhibition in Paris, France.

2012 Saudi Arabia allows its female athletes to compete in the Olympics for the first time.

1992 Shaquille O'Neal is chosen as the number-one draft pick for the Orlando Magic.

 JAN
 FEB
 MAR
 APR
 MAY
 JUN
 JUL
 AUG
 SEP
 OCT
 NOV
DEC

JUNE 25

1947 Contact Publishing publishes *The Diary of Anne Frank.*

1788 Virginia becomes the tenth state to join the Union.

2009 Singer Michael Jackson dies at age fifty.

1903 Marie Curie announces the discovery of radium.

1977 Roy C. Sullivan becomes the first man to be struck by lightning seven times.

1962 The US Supreme Court prohibits prayer in public schools.

2020 Country music band The Dixie Chicks is renamed The Chicks.

2021 *The Mysterious Benedict Society* premieres on Disney+.

JUNE 26

1974 Baseball great Derek Jeter is born in Pequannock Township, New Jersey.

1997 *Harry Potter and the Philosopher's Stone* goes on sale in the UK.

American troops fight in World War I

1844 John Tyler becomes the first and only US President to elope, marrying Julia Gardiner.

1979 Heavyweight champion Muhammad Ali announces his retirement from boxing.

1977 Elvis Presley performs in public for the last time in Indianapolis, Indiana.

1917 The first US troops arrive in France during World War I.

1973 The musical *Grease* premieres in London.

2012 The animated film *Ice Age: Continental Drift* premieres in Buenos Aires.

 JUNE 27

 JAN
 FEB
 MAR
APR
 MAY
 JUN
JUL
 AUG
 SEP
OCT
NOV
DEC

JAN
 FEB
MAR
APR
MAY
 JUN
 JUL
 AUG
 SEP
 OCT
NOV
DEC

1967 Enfield, London, opens the world's first operating ATM.

1871 The yen becomes the official new currency in Japan.

1927 The English Bulldog becomes the mascot of the US Marines.

2017 Mark Zuckerberg announces that

Facebook has reached two billion monthly users.

2021 Canada records its hottest temperature on record at 116°F.

1970 The rock band Smile is renamed "Queen."

1954 The first nuclear power plant opens in the Soviet Union.

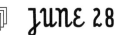 JUNE 28

2005 *Percy Jackson and the Lightning Thief*, by Rick Riordan, is published.

1859 The world's first official dog show is

held in Newcastle On-Tyne, England.

1926 Automakers Meceredes and Benz merge to form Mercedes-Benz.

*Grover
Cleveland
in 1885*

1894 US President Cleveland declares Labor Day a federal holiday.

2007 The bald eagle is removed from the US list of endangered species.

1972 President Nixon announces that no new draftees will be sent to Vietnam.

1976 Women enter the US Air Force for the first time.

1997 Mike Tyson makes boxing history by biting off part of his opponent's ear.

  JUNE 29

2007 Pixar releases *Ratatouille*.

1927 The first US military aircraft make a flight from the West Coast to Hawaii.

 JAN
 FEB
MAR
APR
 MAY
 JUN
 JUL
 AUG
SEP
OCT
NOV
DEC

1613 Shakespeare's Globe of Theater in London catches fire.

1534 Jacques Cartier discovers Prince Edward Island off of Canada.

1888 Frederick Treves performs the first appendectomy in England.

1891 US Congress establishes the National Forest Service.

JUNE 30

1953 Automaker Chevrolet manufacturers its first Corvette.

1894 London officially opens Tower Bridge.

1859 Charles Blondin becomes the first person to walk across Niagara Falls on a tightrope.

1985 Olympic swimmer Michael Phelps is born in Baltimore, Maryland.

1937 The world's first emergency number (9-9-9) is put into use in London.

2017 *Despicable Me 3* opens in theaters.

1975 The Jackson 5 leave Motown records

and change their
name to The Jacksons.

📑 JULY 1

1874 The nation's first zoo opens in Philadelphia.

2003 Tesla motors begins in San Carlos, California.

1961 Diana, Princess of Wales, is born in Sandringham, England.

1963 The US Postal Service begins the use of zip codes.

1904 The U.S. hosts its first Olympic Games in St. Louis, Missouri.

1979 Sony releases its portable music device, the Walkman, in Japan.

Princess Diana in 1996

JUL

JAN

 FEB

MAR

APR

MAY

JUN

JUL

AUG

SEP

OCT

NOV

 DEC

1863 The Battle of Gettysburg begins.

....

 JULY 2

2021 Skulpturparken Blokhus builds the world's tallest sandcastle at 69.5 feet.

....

1962 The first Walmart store opens in Rogers, Arkansas.

....

1998 *Harry Potter and the Chamber of Secrets*, by J. K. Rowling, releases in the UK.

....

2016 Nobel Peace Prize recipient Elie Wiesel dies at age eighty-seven.

....

1979 Susan B. Anthony becomes the first woman depicted on US currency.

....

Susan B. Anthony in 1900 at age eighty

1992 The one-millionth Chevrolet Corvette rolls off the assembly line.

1932 Dave Thomas, the founder of Wendy's hamburgers, is born in Atlantic City, New Jersey.

  JULY 3

1890 Idaho becomes the forty-third state to join the Union.

1985 *Back to the Future* opens in theaters.

1863 The Battle of Gettysburg becomes America's most deadly battle on domestic soil.

1962 Actor Tom Cruise is born in Syracuse, New York.

1987 Richard Branson and Per Lindstrand become the first people to cross the Atlantic in a hot air balloon.

1608 Samuel de Champlain of France discovers Quebec, Canada.

 **JULY 4**

 JAN
 FEB
 MAR
 APR
 MAY
 JUN
 JUL
 AUG
 SEP
OCT
NOV
DEC

JAN
FEB
MAR
APR
MAY
JUN
JUL
AUG
SEP
OCT
NOV
DEC

1960 The new American flag with all fifty stars debuts.

....

1776 The U.S. declares its independence from the British Empire.

....

1848 The cornerstone is laid for America's first national memorial (the Washington Monument).

....

1979 Teresa Salcedo becomes the fifth child born in Disneyland.

....

1934 George Washington's face on Mount Rushmore is completed.

....

1826 Founding fathers Thomas Jefferson and John Adams die on the same day.

....

2019 Anchorage, Alaska, records its hottest-ever temperature at 94°F.

....

2019 California gets hit with its latest earthquake in twenty years (6.4 magnitude) near Ridgecrest.

....

 # JULY 5

1994 Amazon begins in Bellevue, Washington.

....

1687 Sir Isaac Newton publishes his book *Principia* about laws of motion and gravitation.

1958 Bill Watterson, the creator of the cartoon *Calvin and Hobbes*, is born in Washington, D.C.

1943 The largest tank battle of World War II takes place in the Soviet Union and involves 6,000 tanks!

2012 A 51,000-year-old deer bone carving by Neanderthals is found in Germany.

1986 The Statue of Liberty reopens to the public after restoration work.

1643 The first tornado in the U.S. is reported in Essex County, Massachusetts.

The Statue of Liberty in 1955

 JULY 6

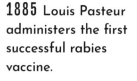

*Anne
Frank*

1942 Anne Frank and her family go into hiding in an attic apartment.

1854 The US Republican party forms in Michigan.

1885 Louis Pasteur administers the first successful rabies vaccine.

1957 Beatles members John Lennon and Paul McCartney meet for the first time (in a long while) at a church party.

2016 Niantic and Nintendo release *Pokémon Go!*

2017 France announces it will ban gas and diesel cars beginning in 2040.

1946 George W. Bush is born in New Haven, Connecticut.

JULY 7

1930 Construction begins on the Hoover Dam in Nevada.

1928 The Chillicothe Baking Company in Missouri introduces pre-sliced bread.

1668 Sir Isaac Newton earns his master's degree from Trinity College in Cambridge, England.

2017 Tesla Motors produces its first Model 3 automobile.

1863 The U.S. issues its first military draft.

1946 Mother Frances Xavier Cabrini becomes the first American saint.

1981 The *Solar Challenger* becomes the first solar-powered aircraft to cross the English Channel.

 # JULY 8

1889 *The Wall Street Journal* publishes its first paper.

1831 John Pemberton, the creator of Coca-Cola, is born in Knoxville, Georgia.

2016 *The Secret Life of Pets* opens in theaters.

1796 The U.S. gives out its first recorded passport.

....

1776 The US Declaration of Independence has its first public reading.

....

2011 US Space Shuttle program launches its final shuttle, *Atlantis*.

....

2000 J. K. Rowling publishes *Harry Potter and the Goblet of Fire*.

....

1996 Spice Girls, the British pop group, releases their single *Wannabe*.

....

 **JULY 9**

2015 Comic-Com in San Diego celebrates its forty-eighth annual event.

....

1958 The tallest-ever recorded wave, measuring 1,720 feet, hits Lituya Bay, Alaska.

....

1981 Nintendo releases its game *Donkey Kong* in Japan.

....

1877 The first Wimbledon Championship is held in London, England.

....

1962 Artist Andy Warhol displays

Tom Hanks in 2017

his artwork for the first time at the Ferus Gallery in Los Angeles.

1956 Oscar-winning actor Tom Hanks is born in Concord, California.

1893 The first successful heart surgery in the U.S. takes place in Chicago.

2009 Joe Sakic retires after twenty-one seasons with the NHL.

📑 JULY 10

1981 Disney releases *The Fox and the Hound* movie.

2019 Automaker Volkswagen ends

production of the Beetle.

1890 Wyoming becomes the forty-fourth state to join the Union.

JAN
FEB
MAR
APR
MAY
JUN
JUL
AUG
SEP
OCT
NOV
DEC

1993 Yobes Ondieki of Kenya becomes the first human to run 10,000 meters (6.2 miles) in under twenty-seven minutes.

....

2018 The final member of the Thailand boy's soccer team is rescued from the Tham Luang Nang Non cave.

....

2019 *Forbes* names Taylor Swift the world's highest-paid entertainer (at $185 million) in 2018.

....

1962 Martin Luther King Jr. is arrested for civil rights demonstrations the previous December.

....

The Martin Luther King Jr. Memorial

JULY 11

1960 Author Harper Lee publishes her first novel, *To Kill a Mockingbird*.

....

1914 Babe Ruth plays his first MLB game for the Red Sox.

1934 Franklin D. Roosevelt becomes the first US president to travel through the Panama Canal.

1976 Austria forms its first football club.

1977 Martin Luther King Jr. receives the US Medal of Freedom posthumously.

1991 Hawaii experiences a total solar eclipse.

2011 The planet Neptune completes its first orbit since its initial discovery in 1846.

JULY 12

1957 The US Surgeon General reports that there is a direct link between smoking and lung cancer.

2017 South Korean pop group MXM forms.

1976 The game show *Family Feud* debuts on ABC.

2018 The world's longest fingernails, measuring 909.6 cm, get trimmed!

JAN FEB MAR APR MAY JUN JUL AUG SEP OCT NOV DEC

JAN
 FEB
MAR
 APR
MAY
 JUN
JUL
AUG
SEP
OCT
NOV
 DEC

1997 Human rights activist and Nobel Prize recipient Malala Yousafzai is born in Pakistan.

1957 President Dwight Eisenhower becomes the first US president to fly in a helicopter.

1962 The Rolling Stones forms in London, England.

1960 The Etch-A-Sketch debuts.

JULY 13

1937 The first Krispy Kreme store opens in Winston-Salem, North Carolina.

1993 The first Chipotle restaurant opens in Denver, Colorado.

1923 Erno Rubik, the inventor of the Rubik's cube, is born in Budapest, Hungary.

1977 New York City experiences one of its worst blackouts, which lasts twenty-five hours!

1923 Iconic Hollywood sign is installed in Hollywood Hills, Los Angeles.

1863 Riots break out in New York City to protest the Civil War military draft.

An illustration of John F. Kennedy

1960 John F. Kennedy is nominated as the Democratic presidential candidate.

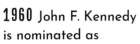 **JULY 14**

2013 The world's last telegram is sent in India.

1864 Gold is discovered in Helena, Montana.

1927 The first commercial flight is made to Hawaii.

1975 Plans for the EPCOT Center in Florida are announced.

1983 Nintendo releases *Mario Bros* in Japan.

2015 Harper Lee's second novel, *Go Set a Watchman*, goes on sale.

 JAN
 FEB
 MAR
 APR
 MAY
 JUN
 JUL
 AUG
 SEP
 OCT
 NOV
 DEC

JAN
 FEB
 MAR
 APR
 MAY
 JUN
 JUL
 AUG
 SEP
 OCT
NOV
DEC

2020 A study announces that the Andean condor bird can fly five hours without flapping its wings.

📑 JULY 15

1799 French Captain Pierre-Francois discovers the Rosetta Stone.

1904 Los Angeles becomes home to the first Buddhist temple in the U.S.

1922 The Bronx Zoological Park exhibits the first duck-billed platypus in the U.S.

1870 Georgia becomes the last state to be readmitted to the Union after the Civil War.

1916 William Boeing, an aviation pioneer, forms the Boeing Company.

A Boeing 737 prepares to land

2005 Disneyland theme park gets a star on the Hollywood Walk of Fame.

1957 Ford Motor Company begins production of the 1958 Edsel, one the biggest product failures in automotive history.

 # JULY 16

1769 Father Serra founds Mission San Diego de Alcala, the first mission in California.

1935 The world's first parking meters are installed in Oklahoma City, Oklahoma.

1945 The U.S. tests its first atomic bomb near Alamogordo, New Mexico.

1969 NASA's *Apollo 11* launches for the moon from the Kennedy Space Center.

1902 The first modern electric air conditioner is installed in Brooklyn, New York.

1439 England bans kissing to stop the spread of the Black Death.

2005 *Harry Potter and the Half-Blood Prince* goes on sale, selling nine million

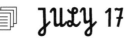

copies in just twenty-four hours.

📑 JULY 17

1989 Disneyland's Splash Mountain opens in California.

1955 Arco, Idaho, becomes the first town to be entirely powered by atomic energy.

1955 Disneyland opens in Anaheim, California.

2019 Netflix streaming service reaches 150 million subscribers.

2015 Marvel's *Ant-Man* movie opens in theaters.

1948 US Air Force pilots drop candy for children in Berlin during the Berlin Blockade.

📑 JULY 18

2012 See's Candies creates the largest lollipop in the world at 7,003 pounds.

A World War II German stamp featuring Adolph Hitler

1925 Adolf Hitler publishes *Mein Kampf*.

1918 Antiapartheid activist Nelson Mandela is born in South Africa.

1976 Nadia Comaneci becomes the first gymnast to receive a perfect score in an Olympics.

1817 English novelist Jane Austin dies at age forty-one.

1980 Actress Kristen Bell, the voice of Anna in *Frozen*, is born in Michigan.

1994 Crayola introduces scented crayons.

𝒥𝓊𝓛𝓎 19

1903 Bicyclist Maurice Garin wins the first Tour de France race.

1894 Inventor of the microwave oven, Percy Spencer, is born in Howland, Maine.

1848 The first-ever women's rights convention is held in Seneca Falls, New York.

1991 MLB legend Cal Ripkin Jr. plays in his 1,500th consecutive game.

1996 Summer Olympic Games open in Atlanta, Georgia.

2018 Painted to look like a whale, the Airbus Beluga XL makes its first flight.

2021 Known as "Freedom Day," the UK lifts most COVID-19 restrictions.

Cal Ripken Jr. in 2013

 JULY 20

1969 Neil Armstrong becomes the first man to walk on the moon.

1968 The first Special Olympics is held at Chicago's Soldier Field.

2021 Jeff Bezos goes to space in his company's Blue Origin rocket.

1921 Alice Mary Robertson becomes the first congresswoman to preside over the floor of the House of Representatives.

1926 The Methodist Church allows women to become priests.

1976 MLB player Hank Aaron hits his last home run.

1927 Charles Lindbergh begins his US tour, stopping in every state with his plane *The Spirit* of St. Louis.

JAN FEB MAR APR MAY JUN JUL AUG SEP OCT NOV DEC

JULY 21

2017 The video game *Fortnite* is released.

2014 Marvel's *Guardians of the Galaxy* premieres in Hollywood, Los Angeles.

2007 J. K. Rowling publishes *Harry Potter and the Deathly*

Hallows, the final book in her record-breaking Harry Potter series.

1861 The Battle of Bull Run begins, marking the first major battle of the Civil War.

1853 Hundreds of acres of land in Manhattan are set aside for making Central Park.

1983 Vostok, Antarctica, sets the record for the coldest day in recorded history at -128.6°F.

2013 Chris Froome of Great Britain wins the 100th Tour de France.

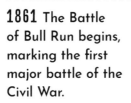

JULY 22

1893 Katharine Lee Bates pens her famous song *America the Beautiful*.

1587 English settlers arrive at Roanoke Island off the coast of North Carolina.

1940 Emmy-winning game show host Alex Trebek is born in Ontario, Canada.

2019 The Dallas Cowboys are named the world's most valuable sports team at a worth of $5 billion.

A standup promotion for Avengers: Endgame

2019 Marvel's *Avengers: Endgame* becomes the highest-grossing film to date.

1923 MLB pitcher Walter Johnson becomes the first to strike out 3,000 batters.

1955 Richard Nixon becomes the first US vice president to preside over a cabinet meeting.

  JULY 23

1715 Permission is granted for the first US lighthouse to be built at Little Brewster Island.

1827 Francis Lieber and Charles Follen establish the first swimming school and pool in Boston.

2010 Pop group One Direction forms in London, England.

 JAN
 FEB
 MAR
 APR
 MAY
 JUN
 JUL
 AUG
 SEP
 OCT
 NOV
DEC

1903 Dentist Ernest Pfennig becomes the first owner of a Ford Model A automobile.

2020 China begins its first mission to Mars

2015 NASA announces its discovery of an Earth-like planet located 1,400 light-years away.

1877 Hawaii gets its first telephone and telegraph line.

1829 Willam Austin Burt patents the first typewriter.

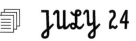

JULY 24

1956 Comedy team Dean Martin and Jerry Lewis perform their last act together.

2020 American TV show host and personality Regis Philbin dies at age eighty-eight.

Regis Philbin receives the 2,222 star on the Hollywood Walk of Fame in 2003

1897 Aviator Amelia Earhart is born in Atchison, Kansas.

....

2018 Bison calves are born in Banff National Park, Alberta, for the first time in 140 years.

....

1982 Music single *Eye of the Tiger* by Survivor reaches number one on the Billboard Hot 100.

....

1975 Giorgio Armani founds his own designer fashion brand in Milan, Italy.

....

1847 Pioneers of the Church of Jesus Christ of Latter-day Saints first arrive in Salt Lake City, Utah.

....

JULY 25

1978 Louise Joy Brown, the first successful in-vitro fertilization baby, is born in England.

....

2007 India elects its first female president, Pratibha Patil.

....

2016 Verizon Wireless buys Yahoo for $4.8 billion.

....

1868 US Congress forms the Wyoming Territory.

....

1850 Gold is discovered in the

JAN
FEB
MAR
APR
MAY
JUN

JUL

AUG

SEP
OCT
NOV
DEC

JAN
FEB
MAR
APR
MAY
JUN
JUL
AUG
SEP
OCT
NOV
DEC

Rogue River in Oregon.

1985 Steve Cram runs the world's fastest mile in 3 minutes and 46 seconds.

 # JULY 26

1951 Disney releases *Alice in Wonderland* in London.

1788 New York becomes the eleventh state to join the Union.

1990 The Americans with Disabilities Act is signed into law.

1948 By Executive Order 9981, President Truman abolishes racial segregation in the U.S. military.

1775 Benjamin Franklin becomes the first postmaster general of the US Postal Service.

2017 Great Britain announces a ban on diesel and gas-powered cars by 2040.

1946 Honolulu International Airport begins its Aloha Airline service.

1908 The Bureau of Investigation, later called the FBI, begins.

JULY 27

1869 Amos Tyler of Toledo receives a patent for chewing gum.

1987 French explorers recover the first artifacts from the *Titanic*.

1938 Gary Gygax, co-creator of *Dungeons & Dragons*, is born in Chicago, Illinois.

1999 Skateboarding legend Tony Hawk lands the first "900" at the fifth annual X Games.

1909 Orville Wright stays aloft in an airplane for one hour, twelve minutes, and forty seconds.

1988 Boston has its worst traffic jam in thirty years.

2003 Comedian Bob Hope dies at age 100.

JULY 28

1914 World War I officially begins.

2017 The *Emoji Movie* opens in theaters.

2005 The Irish Republican Army announces it will end operations.

1943 IKEA opens its first store in Sweden.

2019 Kyle Giersdorf wins the first-ever Fortnite World Cup.

📑 JULY 29

1921 Adolf Hitler is named president of the Nazi party.

2005 Astronomers discover the dwarf planet Eris.

1981 Prince Charles and Lady Diana

Spencer marry in London.

1907 Sir Robert Baden-Powell starts the Boy Scouts in England.

1954 J. R. R. Tolkien publishes *The Lord*

Bag End movie set created for the Lord of the Rings movies

of the Rings: The Fellowship of the Ring.

1883 Italian dictator Benito Mussolini is born.

1836 Arc de Triomphe in Paris becomes the largest triumphal arch in the world.

1927 The first iron lung to treat polio is installed in Bellevue Hospital in New York City.

 # JULY 30

1909 Eugene Schueller forms the beauty company that will eventually become L'Oreal.

1965 Medicare and Medicaid begin in the U.S.

1990 Automaker Saturn produces its first car.

2018 Flight MH370 from Malaysia Airlines goes missing.

2021 Amazon becomes the second-biggest employer in the U.S. (the first is Walmart).

1947 Arnold Schwarzenegger, the famous bodybuilder, actor, and politician, is born in Thal, Austria.

JAN
FEB
MAR
APR
MAY
JUN
JUL
AUG
SEP
OCT
NOV
DEC

📑 JULY 31

2016 American Olympic swimmer Michael Phelps wins his last gold medal.

1965 Author J. K. Rowling is born in England.

1995 Disney acquires Capital Cities, ABC, and ESPN for $19 billion.

1971 The Lunar Rover takes its first drive on the Moon's surface.

1498 Christopher Columbus comes across the island of Trinidad.

1969 The first pictures of Mars are captured by the *Mariner 6* space probe.

📑 AUGUST 1

1876 Colorado becomes the thirty-eighth state to join the Union.

1973 Cable cars in San Francisco make their first run.

2018 The crown jewels of Sweden are stolen in broad daylight.

1996 The US women's soccer team wins its first Olympic gold medal.

Cable cars in present-day San Francisco

1981 MTV debuts as the first twenty-four-hour music channel.

1936 The first televised Olympic games are broadcast from Germany.

1944 Anne Frank writes her last diary entry.

AUGUST 2

2018 Tik Tok service becomes available worldwide.

1858 In Boston, Massachusetts, mail is collected from mailboxes for the first time.

1790 The first US census begins collecting population data.

1909 The first US pennies depicting Abraham Lincoln are put into circulation.

 JAN
 FEB
MAR
APR
 MAY
JUN
 JUL
 AUG
 SEP
OCT
 NOV
DEC

JAN
 FEB
MAR
 APR
MAY
JUN
JUL
 AUG
SEP
OCT
NOV
DEC

1834 Frederic Auguste Bartholdi, the designer of the Statue of Liberty, is born in France.

1992 Jackie Joyner-Kersee wins the heptathlon in back-to-back Olympic games

1993 Rocket *Titan IV* explodes after launching from Vandenberg Air Force Base, California.

AUGUST 3

1975 The New Orleans Superdome arena opens.

1914 The *SS Cristobal* makes its first unofficial pass through the Panama Canal.

1977 NFL star Tom Brady is born in San Mateo, California.

A modern-day crop duster in Idaho

1492 Christopher Columbus sets out on his first voyage.

1900 Harry Firestone founds Firestone Tires in Akron, Ohio.

1921 Crop dusting is used for the first time in Ohio to kill caterpillars.

2021 Hawaii experiences its largest wildfire on record.

 # AUGUST 4

2021 *Forbes* names Rihanna the world's wealthiest female musician at $1.7 billion.

1961 US President Barack Obama is born in Honolulu, Hawaii.

1944 The German secret police discover the hidden apartment of Anne Frank's family.

2011 A truck carrying 104 beehives overturns on a highway in Alberta, Canada.

2006 The world's longest hotdog (197 feet!) is made by Shizuoka Meat Producers in Japan.

1979 US President Jimmy Carter establishes the Department of Energy.

1558 The Jewish Kabbalah, Zohar, is printed for the first time.

1936 Jesse Owens wins his second gold medal at the Olympic games in Berlin, Germany.

AUGUST 5

1961 The Six Flags Over Texas amusement park opens in Arlington, Texas.

1914 Cleveland, Ohio, installs the first electric traffic lights in America.

1861 America's first income tax is signed into law by President Lincoln.

1912 Japan's first taxicabs debut in Ginza, Tokyo.

2012 Usain Bolt, a runner from Jamaica,

Stevie Wonder in 2011

wins gold and sets the record for the 100m race at 9.63 seconds.

1975 Stevie Wonder signs a contract with Motown Records for $13 million.

1884 Cornerstones are laid on Bedloe's Island for the Statue of Liberty.

 ## AUGUST 6

1962 Jamaica becomes an independent country after 300 years of British rule.

2015 The world's largest pinball tournament is held in Pittsburgh, Pennsylvania.

2006 Tiger Woods becomes the youngest golfer to win a PGA.

1945 The U.S. drops an atomic bomb on Hiroshima, Japan, to hasten the end of World War II.

1926 At age nineteen, Gertrude Ederle becomes the first woman to swim the English Channel.

1979 Marcus Hooper, at age twelve, becomes the youngest person ever to swim the English Channel.

JAN
FEB
MAR
APR
MAY
JUN
JUL
AUG
SEP
OCT
NOV
DEC

1965 The Beatles release *Help!*, their fifth album.

1960 A worldwide dance craze begins when *The Twist* is played on the *Dick Clark Show*.

AUGUST 7

1985 Stever Bruner creates AirHead candies.

2007 MLB star Barry Bonds hits his 756th career home run.

1888 Theophilus Van Kannal receives a patent for the revolving door.

1782 General George Washington creates the National Badge of Merit (or Purple Heart medal).

1993 Buckingham Palace opens for public tours.

2018 The population of Australia hits twenty-five million.

1992 The Orlando Magic choose Shaquille O'Neal as their number-one NBA draft pick.

AUGUST 8

1974 Richard Nixon resigns as President of the United States.

2000 A Confederate submarine from 1864 is raised from the ocean floor near Sullivans Island, South Carolina.

1998 Singer Shawn Mendez is born in Toronto, Canada.

1854 Smith and Wesson patent the first metal bullet cartridges.

2017 Disney announces plans to create its own streaming service, Disney+.

1876 Thomas Edison receives a patent for autographic printing.

1929 *Graf Zeppelin*, the German airship, begins its flight around the world.

 # AUGUST 9

1945 US military drops a second atomic bomb, this time on the Japanese city of Nagasaki.

1173 Construction begins on the Leaning Tower of Pisa in Italy.

1969 Disneyland's Haunted Mansion ride opens in California.

JAN

FEB

MAR

APR

MAY

JUN

JUL

AUG

SEP

OCT

NOV

DEC

1974 Gerald Ford becomes the thirty-eighth US president after Nixon's resignation.

1859 Otis Tufts patents the first elevator in the U.S.

1997 Country star Tim McGraw releases his hit single *Just to See You Smile*.

1971 MLB pitcher Satchel Paige is inducted into the Baseball Hall of Fame.

🗐 AUGUST 10

Ruth Bader Ginsburg during her Senate confirmation hearing

1993 Ruth Bader Ginsburg becomes the second woman to serve on the US Supreme Court.

1846 The US Congress establishes the Smithsonian Institute in Washington, D.C.

1793 The world-famous Louvre museum opens in Paris.

1937 Canon, the world's largest camera manufacturer, begins in Tokyo, Japan.

1821 Missouri becomes the twenty-fourth state to join the Union.

1966 The US Treasury discontinues the $2 bill.

2017 A 100-year-old preserved fruit cake is discovered in Antarctica in an old explorer's hut.

1889 Charles B. Darrow, the inventor of Monopoly, is born in Cumberland, Maryland.

 ## AUGUST 11

1950 Steve Wozniak, co-founder at Apple, is born in San Jose, California.

1989 NASA's Voyager 2 discovers two partial rings around Neptune.

2016 Scientists discover the oldest

JAN
FEB
MAR
APR
MAY
JUN
JUL
AUG
SEP
OCT
NOV
DEC

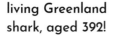

Steve Wozniak in 2014

living Greenland shark, aged 392!

. . . .

1866 Rhode Island opens the world's first skating rink.

. . . .

1885 Public donations totaling $100,000 are

requested to construct a pedestal for the Statue of Liberty.

. . . .

1909 The first "S-O-S" emergency signal is sent off the coast of Cape Hatteras, North Carolina.

. . . .

 AUGUST 12

1990 The most complete and well-preserved T. Rex skeleton, "Sue," is found in South Dakota.

. . . .

1981 Computer company IBM releases its first personal computer.

. . . .

1908 Ford Motors completes its first

Model T automobile in Detroit, Michigan.

1896 Gold is discovered near Dawson City, Yukon Territory, Canada.

1851 Isaac Singer receives a patent for his commercial sewing machine.

1877 American astronomer Asaph Hall discovers Deimos, one of Mars's moons.

2013 The first episode of the animated series *Paw Patrol* airs.

2015 Archeologists discover a mass grave from the 1665 plague at Liverpool Street Station in London.

 # AUGUST 13

2004 Beloved cooking personality Julia Child dies at age ninety-one.

1889 William Gray patents the first coin-operated telephone.

1961 Construction begins on a wall to divide West Berlin from East Germany.

1899 Film director Sir Alfred Hitchcock is born in London.

JAN
FEB
MAR
APR
MAY
JUN
JUL
AUG
SEP
OCT
NOV
DEC

2004 The twenty-eighth Olympic Games returns home to Athens, Greece.

1997 Microsoft releases Internet Explorer 3.0.

1889 Hanson Goodrich patents the stove-top coffee pot.

AUGUST 14

The Cologne Cathedral

1880 The construction of the Cologne Cathedral in Germany is finally completed after 632 years.

1945 Japan surrenders and World War II comes to an end.

1965 *I Got You Babe,* by Sonny and Cher, reaches number one on the music billboards.

1935 The US Social Security program begins.

1945 Actor Steve Martin is born in Waco, Texas.

 ## AUGUST 15

2001 Astronomers announce the discovery of a solar system outside our own.

1914 The Panama Canal officially opens.

1483 The Vatican's Sistine Chapel opens.

1843 Tivoli Gardens, the second-oldest theme park in the world, opens in Copenhagen, Denmark.

2013 A scientist discovers the olinguito, a mammal in the raccoon family.

1989 Joe Jonas, of the Jonas Brothers, is born in Casa Grande, Arizona.

1995 Los del Rio, a Spanish pop duo, release their hit single *Macarena* in the U.S.

1620 The *Mayflower* sets sail from England, only to return shortly because its sister ship, the *Speedwell*, begins taking on water. (The *Mayflower* would

 JAN
 FEB
MAR
 APR
 MAY
 JUN
 JUL
AUG
 SEP
OCT
 NOV
DEC

JAN
FEB
MAR
APR
MAY
JUN
JUL
AUG
SEP
OCT
NOV
DEC

A replica of the Mayflower

eventually undertake the journey on its own.)

AUGUST 16

1955 Disneyland opens its Dumbo the Flying Elephant ride in California.

1954 The first issue of *Sports Illustrated* hits the stands.

1948 Baseball legend Babe Ruth dies at age fifty-three.

2016 Heavy-weight lifting champion Lasha Talakhadze sets a new world record of over one thousand pounds!

1898 Inventor Edwin Prescott receives a patent for his loop roller coaster.

1999 The first episode of *Who Wants to Be a*

Millionaire debuts on ABC.

2019 Rotterdam, Netherlands, opens the world's first floating dairy farm.

1988 IBM introduces artificial intelligence software.

 # AUGUST 17

2008 Michael Phelps becomes the first person to win eight gold medals at a single Olympic Games.

1988 The FDA approves the first hair growth drug, Rogaine.

1786 Legendary frontiersman Davy Crockett is born in Limestone, Tennessee.

2020 University of North Carolina at Chapel Hill becomes the first college to switch to online classes due to COVID-19.

2017 The animated series *Phineas and Ferb* debuts on the Disney Channel.

1966 NASA launches the *Pioneer 7* satellite.

1908 San Francisco opens the Bank of Italy (later to become Bank of America).

JAN
FEB
MAR
APR
MAY
JUN
JUL
AUG
SEP
OCT
NOV
DEC

An illustration of Mars with both its moons

1877 Astronomer Asaph Hall discovers Mars's second moon, Phobos.

 **AUGUST 18**

1998 Mrs. Fields's Cookies announces it will buy the Great American Cookie Company.

1992 NBA all-star Larry Bird announces his retirement.

1939 *The Wizard of Oz* premieres in New York City.

2018 Archeologists discover the world's oldest cheese (3,200 years old!) in an ancient Egyptian tomb.

1949 Adi Dassler establishes the Adidas company.

1963 James Meredith becomes the first African American

to graduate from the University of Mississippi.

1872 Montgomery Ward issues its first mail-order catalog.

 ## AUGUST 19

1856 Gail Borden receives a patent for his method of making evaporated milk.

1946 US President Bill Clinton is born in Hope, Arkansas.

2004 Google Inc. begins selling stock on NASDAQ.

2009 The entrepreneurial show *Shark Tank* debuts on ABC.

2020 Apple becomes the first US company to be worth $2 trillion.

1993 Toy companies Fisher-Price and Mattel merge.

1849 The *New York Herald* newspaper reports gold in California.

1871 American aviator Orville Wright is born in Dayton, Ohio.

AUGUST 20

 JAN
 FEB
 MAR
 APR
 MAY
 JUN
 JUL
 AUG
 SEP
 OCT
 NOV
 DEC

Kamala Harris is sworn in as vice-president in 2021

1989 *Saved by the Bell* debuts on NBC.

2021 Animated film *Paw Patrol: The Movie* opens in theaters.

2020 Kamala Harris accepts the nomination as vice-president.

1913 Adolphe Pegoud becomes the first parachutist to jump from a plane and land safely.

1920 The National Football League has its official beginning

2014 Known for popularizing yoga, Indian teacher B.K.S. Iyengar dies at age ninety-five.

1977 NASA launches the *Voyager 2* spacecraft to study Jupiter, Saturn, Uranus, and Neptune.

AUGUST 21

1942 Disney releases *Bambi*.

1959 Hawaii becomes the fiftieth state to join the Union.

2017 For the first time in almost forty years, the continental U.S. experiences a total solar eclipse.

1911 The famous painting *Mona Lisa* is stolen from the Louvre.

1966 The Beatles perform at the first-ever concert held at the Busch Memorial Stadium.

1972 The first hot air balloon flight over the Swiss Alps takes off.

1985 Mary Decker Slaney sets a world record for the fastest female mile time of just over four minutes.

2019 Dwayne "The Rock" Johnson is named the highest-paid actor for the second year in a row.

 # AUGUST 22

1865 William Sheppard receives a patent for liquid soap.

1989 Scientists discover the first complete ring around Neptune.

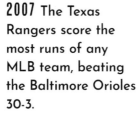

The Volkswagen Rabbit

2007 The Texas Rangers score the most runs of any MLB team, beating the Baltimore Orioles 30-3.

1902 Theodore Roosevelt becomes the first US President to ride in an automobile.

1902 Cadillac Motors begins in Detroit, Michigan.

1989 MLB pitcher Nolan Ryan strikes out his 5,000th batter.

1984 The last Volkswagen Rabbit auto rolls off the line.

1950 Althea Gibson becomes the first black woman to play in a US national tennis competition.

AUGUST 23

1978 NBA legend Kobe Bryant is born in Philadelphia.

2000 The first season of hit reality television show *Survivor* ends.

1904 Harry Weed receives a patent for his automobile tire chains.

1933 The first televised boxing match airs on BBC-TV.

1947 The first Little League World Series takes place in Williamsport, Pennsylvania.

2007 US product designer Chris Messina invents the hashtag.

2015 A twelve-year-old trips at an art exhibit in Taiwan and rips a 17th-century painting worth $1.5 million.

2017 After unexpected rainfall, the world's driest place, the Atacama desert in Chile, blooms.

The Atacama Desert, the driest desert (nonpolar) in the world

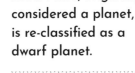 AUGUST 24

1869 Cornelius Swartwout receives a patent for the waffle iron.

79 Mt. Vesuvius erupts, burying the city of Pompeii in fiery ash.

1954 Congress outlaws the Communist Party in the U.S.

2006 Pluto, originally considered a planet, is re-classified as a dwarf planet.

2021 Beyoncé becomes the first Black woman to wear the Tiffany Diamond in an advertising role.

2019 Victor Vescovo of the U.S. becomes the first person to visit the deepest point of every ocean.

2017 The largest US Powerball Jackpot lottery is won at $758.7 million.

2006 NFL legend Jerry Rice retires.

 AUGUST 25

1940 The first parachute wedding ceremony takes place

at the New York City World's Fair.

1989 NASA's *Voyager 2* sends photographs of Neptune and its moon.

1916 The US National Park Service begins.

1609 Astronomer Galileo Galilei

demonstrates his first telescope.

1958 The first package of instant ramen hits the market.

2020 The World Health Organization announces the eradication of polio from Africa.

📄 AUGUST 26

1996 The first Raising Cane's restaurant opens in Baton Rouge, Louisiana.

1910 Mother Teresa of Calcutta is born.

1980 *Home Alone* star Macaulay Culkin

is born in New York City.

2014 Burger King purchases Tim Hortons for $11.4 billion.

2012 Lydia Ko becomes the youngest

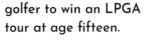

Halley's Comet in 1986 (the last time it appeared)

golfer to win an LPGA tour at age fifteen.

1968 The Beatles release their hit single *Hey Jude*.

1682 Astronomer Edmond Halley discovers a comet and names it after himself: Halley's Comet.

1959 The British Motor Company introduces the Morris Mini-Minor auto.

AUGUST 27

1964 Disney releases its first *Mary Poppins* movie.

1942 The first US Navy ship with a bathtub launches (the *USS Iowa*).

1955 The Guinness Book of Records publishes its first book.

1908 Lyndon B. Johnson, thirty-sixth US president, is born near Stonewall, Texas.

. . . .

1993 Construction on Japan's Rainbow Bridge comes to completion.

. . . .

2011 Hurricane Irene makes landfall in North Carolina.

. . . .

2008 Barack Obama becomes the first African American to be nominated for US president.

. . . .

📑 *AUGUST 28*

1963 Martin Luther King Jr. delivers his famous "I Have A Dream" speech.

. . . .

1928 Charles Brannock receives a

patent for his popular shoe measuring device.

. . . .

2020 *Black Panther* movie actor Chadwick

A Subway sandwich shop in Thailand in 2019

 JAN
 FEB
 MAR
 APR
 MAY
 JUN
 JUL
 AUG
 SEP
 OCT
 NOV
 DEC

JAN
FEB
MAR
APR
MAY
JUN
JUL
AUG
SEP
OCT
NOV
DEC

Boseman dies at age forty-three.

1884 F. N. Robinson takes the first photo of a tornado near Howard, South Dakota.

1965 Bridgeport, Connecticut, opens the first Subway sandwich shop.

 # AUGUST 29

1898 Frank and Charles Seiberling start Goodyear Tires in Akron, Ohio.

2005 Hurricane Katrina makes landfall in Louisiana.

1958 Music legend Michael Jackson is born in Gary, Indiana.

1966 The Beatles give their last concert in Candlestick Park in San Francisco.

1997 Entrepreneurs Reed Hastings and Marc Randolph start Netflix.

1896 Chinese ambassador Li Hung Chang invents chop suey.

1813 American animal rights activist and founder of the ASPCA, Henry Bergh, is born in New York City.

AUGUST 30

1983 The Eiffel Tower receives its 150 millionth visitor.

1983 Guion Bluford Jr. becomes the first African American astronaut.

2021 America ends its twenty-year war in Afghanistan.

1997 The Houston Comets beat the New York Liberty in the first WNBA Championship.

1901 British engineer Hubert Booth files for a patent for his powered vacuum cleaner.

1850 Honolulu, Hawaii, officially becomes a city.

1862 Confederate soldiers win the Second Battle of Bull Run.

1991 American Mike Powell sets a long jump then-record of 29 feet and 4.25 inches.

AUGUST 31

Ken Griffey Jr. in 2019

1997 Princess Diana of Wales dies in a car accident at age thirty-six.

1935 Indianapolis hosts the first national skeet tournament.

1798 The first US bank robbery takes place at the Bank of Pennsylvania.

1904 George C. Poage becomes the first African American to win an Olympic medal.

1899 The first automobile makes it to the top of Mount Washington in New Hampshire.

1990 Ken Griffey and Ken Griffey Jr. become the first father-son duo to play MLB on the same team simultaneously (Seattle Mariners).

𝄞 SEPTEMBER 1

1985 Scientists discover the wreckage of the *Titanic*.

....

1952 Published copies of Hemingway's *The Old Man and the Sea* are released.

....

1914 The last known passenger pigeon dies at the Cincinnati Zoo in Ohio.

....

1904 Helen Keller graduates from Radcliffe College with honors.

....

1939 World War II officially begins in Europe; the U.S. would join two years later.

....

1968 The first US school for training circus clowns opens in Venice, Florida.

....

2021 International soccer star Cristiano Ronaldo breaks the world record for the total number of goals scored.

....

2020 With hit single *Dynamite*, BTS becomes the first all-

An 1878 illustration of the passenger pigeon

JAN
FEB
MAR
APR
MAY
JUN
JUL
AUG
SEP
OCT
NOV
DEC

Korean pop group to top the Billboard 100 chart.

📑 SEPTEMBER 2

1979 California's Disneyland opens the Big Thunder Mountain Railroad ride.

1957 The world's shortest professional boxing match lasts only seven seconds (Teddy Barker vs. Bob Roberts).

1963 *CBS Evening News* becomes the first half-hour weeknight news broadcast.

2015 A study by Yale University claims there are over three trillion trees on the Earth.

1666 Much of London is destroyed in the Great Fire of London.

1945 Vietnam declares independence from France.

1973 Author J. R. R. Tolkien dies at age eighty-one.

1838 The last Hawaiian monarch, Lili'uokalani, is born in Honolulu.

SEPTEMBER 3

2021 Marvel's *Shang-Chi and the Legend of the Rings* opens in theaters.

1783 The American Revolution ends with the signing of the Treaty of Paris.

1967 Driving in Sweden changes from the left side of the road to the right side.

2015 Chandra Bahadur Dangi, the world's shortest man on record at 1 foot and 9.5 inches, dies at age seventy-five.

1609 Henry Hudson sails into the harbor of present-day New York City, naming it the Hudson River.

1995 Pierre Omidyar founds eBay in San Jose, California.

2017 The largest postwar World War II bomb is found in Frankfurt, Germany, and defused.

 # SEPTEMBER 4

1877 In Ravenna, Ohio, the Quaker Oats Company is founded.

 JAN
FEB
MAR
APR
 MAY
 JUN
 JUL
AUG
SEP
OCT
 NOV
DEC

Steve Irwin in 2003

1972 Bob Barker hosts the debut episode of the revamped *The Price is Right*.

1781 Spanish settlers found Los Angeles.

2006 Steve Irwin, the Australian host of *The Crocodile Hunter*, dies at age forty-four.

2002 Kelly Clarkson becomes the first winner of the reality television show *American Idol*.

1998 Stanford University students Larry Page and Sergey Brin found Google.

1950 Comic strip *Beetle Bailey* by Mort Walker debuts in newspapers.

SEPTEMBER 5

1946 Freddy Mercury, lead singer of the rock band Queen, is born in Tanzania.

1997 Mother Teresa of Calcutta dies at age eighty-seven.

1976 The first episode of *The Muppet Show* airs.

1666 The Great Fire of London ends after destroying 13,200 homes.

1984 The space shuttle *Discovery* lands after its maiden voyage.

1949 Chemist Willard Frank Libby announces the discovery of radiocarbon dating.

1906 Bradbury Robinson completes the first forward pass in football.

A depiction of the 1666 Great London Fire

JAN
FEB
MAR
APR
MAY
JUN
JUL
AUG
SEP
OCT
NOV
DEC

SEPTEMBER 6

1997 Elton John sings *Candle in the Wind* at the funeral of Princess Diana.

2017 Hurricane Irma makes landfall in Barbuda, Sint Maartens, and the British Virgin Islands.

1716 The first North American lighthouse is built in Boston.

1869 The first US westbound train arrives in San Francisco.

1916 Clarence Saunder opens the first true supermarket, the Piggly Wiggly, in Memphis, Tennessee.

1995 Cal Ripkin Jr. plays his 2,131st consecutive MLB game, surpassing the previous record by Lou Gehrig.

1979 National Grandparents Day is first observed.

SEPTEMBER 7

1630 Boston becomes the new name for Trimountaine, Massachusetts.

1888 The first incubator is used for a premature infant.

1979 The Entertainment and Sports Programming Network (ESPN) debuts.

1963 The Pro Football Hall of Fame opens in Canton, Ohio.

2014 Serena Williams wins her third straight US tennis title.

2005 Egypt holds its first presidential election.

1916 US Congress passes the Workmen's Compensation Act.

 ## SEPTEMBER 8

1921 Margaret Gorman wins the first Miss America pageant.

1966 Television show *Star Trek* debuts on NBC.

1892 The US Pledge of Allegiance is first published.

1930 Company 3M begins marketing its transparent adhesive tape (soon to be called "Scotch tape").

Immigrants arrive at Ellis Island in 1910

1504 Michelangelo's statue of David goes on display in Florence, Italy.

1986 The first national broadcast of *The Oprah Winfrey Show* takes place.

1990 New York City opens the Ellis Island Historical Site.

SEPTEMBER 9

1776 The Continental Congress renames the "United Colonies" the "United States."

1850 California becomes the thirty-first state to join the Union.

2015 Queen Elizabeth II becomes the longest-reigning monarch in British history.

. . . .

1990 Tennis great Pete Sampras wins his first of fourteen Grand Slam titles.

. . . .

1966 Comedian and actor Adam Sandler is born in Brooklyn, New York.

. . . .

1890 John Boyd Dunlop receives a patent for his air-pressurized rubber tire.

. . . .

2021 NFL quarterback Tom Brady becomes the first player in history to start 300 regular-season games.

. . . .

 # SEPTEMBER 10

1990 The first episode of *The Fresh Prince of Bellaire* debuts.

. . . .

1994 *The Magic School Bus* television show airs its first episode.

. . . .

1623 Furs and lumber are the first cargo sent back to England from North America.

. . . .

1913 The Lincoln Highway becomes the first paved, coast-to-coast highway in the U.S.

. . . .

 JAN
 FEB
 MAR
 APR
 MAY
 JUN
 JUL
 AUG
SEP
 OCT
 NOV
DEC

Alex Trebek in 2006

1984 Alex Trebek hosts his first episode of *Jeopardy!*

....

2013 Apple releases its iTunes Radio music streaming service.

....

2018 California commits to carbon-free electricity sources by 2045.

....

2020 California's August Complex wildfire becomes the largest fire in state history.

....

📑 SEPTEMBER 11

1916 For the first time, *The Star-Spangled Banner* is sung to start a baseball game.

....

1941 Construction begins on the US Pentagon.

....

2001 The US World Trade Center and

Pentagon are attacked by terrorists.

1928 The first transcontinental bus service begins from New York to Los Angeles.

1977 The Atari gaming systems debuts.

1974 Television show *Little House on the Prairie* premieres on NBC.

2002 All-time great quarterback Johnny Unitas dies at age sixty-nine.

 # SEPTEMBER 12

1962 The first Kohl's retail chain opens in Brookfield, Wisconsin.

2011 The 9/11 Memorial Museum opens in New York City.

1959 Western television show *Bonanza* debuts on NBC.

1910 LAPD hires Alice Stebbins Wells as the first policewoman with power to arrest.

2003 Country music star Johnny Cash dies at age eighty-eight.

1992 Mae Jemison becomes the first African American woman to fly into space.

1940 Filled with prehistoric cave art, the Lascaux Cave is discovered by four teenage boys in France.

📑 SEPTEMBER 13

An illustration from Roald Dahl's "BFG"

1916 British children's author Roald Dahl is born in Llandaff, Wales.

1857 The founder of the Hershey Chocolate Company,

Milton Hershey, is born in Pennsylvania.

1969 Television show *Scooby-Doo, Where Are You!* premieres on CBS.

1970 Gary Muhrcke wins the first New York City Marathon.

1977 General Motors introduces the first US diesel automobiles.

2009 Taylor Swift, Beyonce Knowles, and

Rihanna win the 26th MTV Video Music Awards

1778 Congress establishes New York City as the first official US capital since the Constitution was ratified.

 # SEPTEMBER 14

1901 William L. Murray wins the first bodybuilding contest held in London.

1814 Frances Scott Key pens the poem "The Star-Spangled Banner."

1963 Cathay, Jimmie, Maggie, Margie, and Mary Ann Fischer

become the first US quintuplets.

2021 The U.S. records its lowest levels of poverty since records began in 1967.

1868 Tom Morris makes golf's first recorded hole-in-one in Scotland.

JAN
FEB
MAR
APR
MAY
JUN
JUL
AUG
SEP
OCT
NOV
DEC

JAN

FEB

MAR

APR

MAY

JUN

JUL

AUG

SEP

OCT

NOV

DEC

1901 Theodore Roosevelt becomes the then-youngest US president at age forty-two.

Theodore Roosevelt in 1910

 # SEPTEMBER 15

1983 The first Costco opens its doors in Seattle, Washington.

1984 Prince Harry of Wales is born in London.

1949 *The Lone Ranger* debuts on ABC.

2012 Legoland Malaysia opens to visitors.

1890 British author Agatha Christie is born in Torquay, England.

1996 The Texas Rangers retire their first-ever number: #34 for Nolan Ryan.

1997 Google.com is registered as a domain name.

2019 Television producer Norman Lear becomes the oldest person to win an Emmy at age ninety-seven.

SEPTEMBER 16

1998 Actress Meryl Streep receives her star on the Hollywood Walk of Fame.

1620 The *Mayflower* sets sail (again) from Plymouth, England, carrying 102 pilgrims.

1908 Willam Durant founds General Motors.

1956 American magician David Copperfield is born in Metuchen, New Jersey.

1975 Papua New Guinea gains independence from Australia.

2018 Patrick Mahomes becomes the first NFL player to record ten touchdowns in the first two weeks of a season.

1992 Nick Jonas of the Jonas Brothers is born in Dallas, Texas.

2018 Denise Mueller-Korenek breaks the

record for cycling land speed, riding at 183.93 miles per hour. Wow!

 ## SEPTEMBER 17

2019 Animated show *The Last Kids on Earth* premieres on Netflix.

1954 William Golding publishes his Pulitzer-winning book, *Lord of the Flies.*

1983 Vanessa Williams becomes the first African American woman to be crowned Miss America.

1972 Comedy television show *M*A*S*H* debuts on CBS.

1632 Dutch scientist Anton van Leeuwenhoek discovers bacteria.

1789 Astronomer William Herschel discovered Mimas, a satellite of Saturn.

1849 Harriet Tubman escapes from slavery.

SEPTEMBER 18

The Washington Monument in Washington, D.C.

1793 George Washington lays the cornerstone for the US capitol building in Washington, D.C.

2020 US Supreme Court Justice Ruth Bader Ginsburg dies at age eighty-seven.

1837 Charles Tiffany and John Young establish the luxury jewelry company Tiffany and Co.

1851 The *New York Times* publishes its first issue.

1769 John Harris of Boston builds the first spinet piano.

1964 *The Addams Family* television show debuts on ABC.

 # SEPTEMBER 19

1970 *The Mary Tyler Moore Show* premieres on television.

1999 The Dixie Chicks become the first country music group to top the Billboard charts.

1982 After 122 years of service, streetcars on San Francisco's Market Street stop running.

1893 New Zealand becomes the first country to allow all women the right to vote.

1957 America's first underground nuclear tests are conducted in Nevada.

1876 Melville Bissell patents the first carpet sweeper.

1975 Alligators are no longer listed as an endangered species in parts of Louisiana.

SEPTEMBER 20

President Chester Arthur in 1882

1881 Chester A. Arthur becomes the twenty-first US president.

2017 Hurricane Maria strikes Puerto Rico, causing $90 billion in damage.

2001 President George W. Bush declares a "war on terror" in his address to Congress.

1886 Johannesburg officially becomes a city in South Africa.

1878 American novelist Upton Sinclair is born in Baltimore, Maryland.

1863 Creator of *Grimm's Fairy Tales*, Jakob Ludwig Karl Grimm, dies in Germany at age seventy-eight.

 # SEPTEMBER 21

1970 The Cleveland Browns and the New York Jets play the first game of *Monday Night Football*.

1991 The Huntington Library in California makes photos of the Dead Sea Scrolls available to the public.

1981 Belize gains independence from Britain.

1915 The prehistoric monument Stonehenge is sold at auction for 6,000 pounds (about $1 million today—still a bargain!).

1950 American comedian Bill Murray is born in Evanston, Illinois.

2021 McDonald's announces plans to reduce the amount of plastic used in its Happy Meals.

1937 J.R.R. Tolkien publishes his novel *The Hobbit*.

1991 Armenia gains independence from the USSR.

📑 SEPTEMBER 22

1987 The first episode of *Full House* airs on television.

1915 The first African American Catholic college, Xavier University, opens in New Orleans.

1961 Congress authorizes the creation of the US Peace Corps.

2015 MLB player and coach Yogi Berra dies at age ninety.

Yogi Berra in 2011

1958 Opera singer Andrea Bocelli is born near Pisa, Italy.

 # SEPTEMBER 23

1986 Congress votes that the rose become the official US flower.

1962 ABC airs the first episode of the space-age cartoon *The Jetsons.*

1846 German astronomer Johann Gottfried Galle discovers Neptune.

1962 The New York Philharmonic Hall opens.

1999 Las Vegas duo Siegfried & Roy receive their star on the Hollywood Walk of Fame.

1642 Harvard College in Cambridge, Massachusetts,

JAN
FEB
MAR
APR
MAY
JUN
JUL
AUG
SEP
OCT
NOV
DEC

David Geffen Hall, the present-day home of the New York Philharmonic

holds its first commencement.

. . . .

2002 The first public version of the Mozilla Firefox web browser is made public.

. . . .

1993 At age eleven, Vicki Van Meter becomes the youngest female pilot to fly across the U.S.

. . . .

SEPTEMBER 24

1952 The first Kentucky Fried Chicken restaurant opens in North Corbin, Kentucky.

. . . .

1936 Jim Henson, the creator of the

Muppets, is born in Greenville, Mississippi.

. . . .

1929 Lt. James Doolittle makes the first completely blind airplane takeoff, flight, and landing.

. . . .

1957 Federal troops are sent to Little Rock, Arkansas, to help enforce integration in schools.

1964 *The Munsters* television show debuts on CBS.

1960 The first nuclear-powered aircraft carrier, the *USS Enterprise,* launches from Newport, Virginia.

2016 The US National Museum of African American History and Culture opens in Washington, D.C.

2017 Scientists discover the first plastic rubbish only 1,000 miles from the North Pole.

 ## SEPTEMBER 25

1956 The first transatlantic phone cable lines open between the U.S., Canada, Britain, and Europe.

2015 Columbia Pictures releases *Hotel Transylvania 2*

2016 Famous golfer Arnold Palmer dies at age eighty-seven.

1968 Actor Will Smith is born in Philadelphia.

2020 The African giant pouched rat,

Magawa, receives the PDSA hero award for sniffing out landmines in Cambodia.

2018 Fashion company Michael Kors purchases Versace for $2.1 billion.

1639 The first printing press in America is assembled in Cambridge, Massachusetts.

2012 China's first aircraft carrier begins service.

SEPTEMBER 26

1969 Television show *The Brady Bunch* debuts on ABC.

1960 John F. Kennedy and Richard Nixon present on the first televised US presidential debate.

1981 The Boeing 767 makes its first flight in Everett, Washington.

1969 The Beatles release their last album, *Abbey Road*.

1962 *The Beverly Hillbillies* debuts on CBS.

2020 Amy Coney Barrett is nominated as a Supreme Court Justice.

1993 John David Munday becomes the

Niagara Falls, a drop of 167 feet!

first person to go over Niagara Falls in a barrel twice.

2006 Facebook opens to anyone who is thirteen or older and has a valid email.

 # SEPTEMBER 27

2008 Astronaut Zhai Zhigang becomes China's first man to walk in space.

1995 The redesigned $100 bill is shown publicly for the first time.

1722 American revolutionary Samuel Adams is born in Boston, Massachusetts.

1985 Hurricane Gloria hammers the Atlantic coast with winds of 130 miles per hour.

JAN
FEB
MAR
APR
MAY
JUN
JUL
AUG
SEP
OCT
NOV
DEC

SEP

*Mars
Curiosity
rover*

2012 NASA's *Curiosity* rover discovers evidence of ancient streambeds on Mars.

 **SEPTEMBER 28**

1989 Sony Corporation buys Columbia Pictures for $3.4 billion.

2012 Sony Pictures releases *Hotel Transylvania.*

1542 Explorer Juan Rodriguez Cabrillo lands in San Diego.

1955 The World Series is first broadcast in color by NBC.

1895 Chemist Louis Pasteur is born in France.

2008 SpaceX becomes the first privately owned company to send a liquid-fueled rocket into orbit.

2003 African American tennis great Althea Gibson dies at age seventy-six.

1867 Toronto becomes the official capital of Ontario, Canada.

⎙ SEPTEMBER 29

1829 The British criminal investigation organization, Scotland Yard, is founded.

1966 Chevrolet introduces its soon-to-be-iconic car, the Camaro.

2000 *Remember the Titans* opens in US theaters.

2021 US Fish and Wildlife Service announces the extinction of twenty-three bird, fish, and other wildlife species.

1990 Construction of the Washington National Cathedral is finally completed after eighty-three years.

1936 Radio broadcasts are used for the first time in a presidential campaign.

JAN
FEB
MAR
APR
MAY
JUN
JUL
AUG
SEP
OCT
NOV
DEC

 # SEPTEMBER 30

An illustration depicting a scene from the Magic Flute

1935 President Franklin D. Roosevelt dedicates the Hoover Dam.

1960 Cartoon series *The Flintstones* debuts on ABC.

1975 The US Army's AH-64 Apache helicopter takes its first flight.

1955 American actor James Dean dies at age twenty-four.

1791 Mozart's opera *The Magic Flute* premieres in Vienna.

2004 The first images of a live giant squid in nature are taken 600 miles south of Tokyo.

1997 Microsoft releases Internet Explorer 4.0.

🗐 OCTOBER 1

1908 Ford Motors releases its Ford Model T automobile.

1890 US Congress establishes Yosemite National Park.

1992 The Cartoon Network debuts on television.

1869 Vienna, Austria, issues the world's first postcards.

1924 US President Jimmy Carter is born in Plains, Georgia.

1971 Disney opens the Walt Disney Resort near Orlando, Florida.

1993 *Cool Runnings* debuts in US theaters.

2020 COVID-19 death toll passes 700,000.

🗐 OCTOBER 2

1965 Scientists for the University of Florida invent Gatorade.

2009 County of Los Angeles and City of

Long Beach declare October 2 "Stan Lee Day."

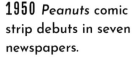

Charlie Brown from "Peanuts"

1950 *Peanuts* comic strip debuts in seven newspapers.

1869 Mahatma Gandhi is born in Porbandar, India.

2017 Rock and Roll singer Tom Petty dies at age sixty-six.

2015 Alphabet Inc. technology conglomerate becomes the parent company of Google.

1992 Disney's *Mighty Ducks* opens in US theaters.

1870 Rome becomes the capital of Italy (it was Turin and Florence before that).

 # OCTOBER 3

1961 The first episode of *The Dick Van Dyke Show* airs on CBS.

....

1952 Great Britain detonates their first atomic bomb.

....

1955 *The Mickey Mouse Club* debuts on ABC.

....

1863 President Lincoln designates the last Thursday in November to be a day of Thanksgiving.

....

2020 The UK records its wettest day ever, averaging 1.24 inches of rain across the country.

....

1996 Tropicana Field becomes the new name of the Thunderdome in Tampa Bay, Florida.

....

 # OCTOBER 4

1999 Sweden celebrates its first Cinnamon Roll Day.

....

1927 Carving begins on the Mount Rushmore Memorial.

....

1957 Family sitcom *Leave It to Beaver* debuts on CBS.

....

1535 The first complete English Bible comes off the printing press.

....

1957 The USSR launches the first artificial satellite, *Sputnik 1*.

2001 The Reagan National Airport in Washington D.C. reopens after 9/11 closures.

2021 Facebook and its apps experience a six-hour global outage.

OCTOBER 5

1921 The baseball World Series is broadcast on the radio for the first time.

2011 Steve Jobs dies at age fifty-six.

1962 The first of the James Bond films, *Dr. No.*, debuts in London.

2005 Stephanie Meyer publishes the first book in her Twilight series.

1961 Audrey Hepburn stars in the movie release of *Breakfast at Tiffany's*.

1975 Actress Kate Winslet is born in Berkshire, England.

1999 MCI Worldcom and Sprint Corporation announce plans to merge.

A poster of Audrey Hepburn

1970 PBS begins broadcasting.

 OCTOBER 6

1993 Michael Jordan retires from the NBA for the first time.

1949 Lonnie Johnson, the inventor of the Super Soaker water gun, is born in Mobile, Alabama.

1848 The SS *California* steamboat leaves New York, bound for San Francisco via Cape Horn.

1961 American families are advised to build or buy bomb shelters in case of a nuclear exchange with the Soviet Union.

1996 Country music stars Faith Hill and Tim McGraw marry.

JAN
FEB
MAR
APR
MAY
JUN
JUL
AUG
SEP
OCT
NOV
DEC

2014 *Alexander and the Terrible, Horrible, No Good, Very Bad Day* movie opens in theaters.

2018 Brett Kavanaugh becomes a US Supreme Court Justice.

2010 Kevin Systrom and Mike Kriger launch Instagram.

📑 OCTOBER 7

Arnold Schwarzenegger as governor in 2004

2003 California elects Arnold Schwarzenegger as governor.

1868 Cornell University welcomes its first students.

1996 The Fox News Channel launches.

1993 Toni Morrison becomes the first Black woman to win the Nobel Prize in Literature.

1959 The first pictures are received of the far side of the moon.

1996 The animated cartoon series *Arthur* debuts on PBS.

2001 The U.S. begins its attack on Afghanistan following 9/11.

1968 The Motion Picture Association of America begins a film-rating system.

OCTOBER 8

1945 The microwave oven receives a patent.

1871 The Peshtigo Fire begins, becoming one of the most devastating wildfires in US history.

1956 New York Yankees pitcher Don Larson pitches the first perfect game in World Series history.

1983 Broadway show *Cats* has its first performance (it would continue for another eighteen years).

JAN FEB MAR APR MAY JUN JUL AUG SEP OCT NOV DEC

2001 President George W. Bush creates the US Department of Homeland Security.

2004 Afghanistan holds its first-ever presidential election.

2019 Montgomery, Alabama, elects Steven Reed, its first Black mayor in over 200 years.

1985 Pop singer Bruno Mars is born in Honolulu, Hawaii.

OCTOBER 9

1776 Spanish settlers dedicate Mission Dolores, the oldest building in San Francisco.

1992 A meteorite strikes a parked car in New York (it is then displayed at the American Museum of Natural History!).

1888 The Washington Monument opens to the public.

1940 Beatles band member John Lennon is born in Liverpool, England.

1949 The Harvard Law School begins admitting women applicants.

Present-day Harvard University

1949 The first electric blanket goes on sale in Petersburg, Virginia, for $39.50.

1983 At age eighty-three, Helen Moss becomes the oldest person to join the Girl Scouts.

OCTOBER 10

1845 The US Naval Academy opens in Annapolis, Maryland.

1865 John Wesley Hyatt patents the billiard ball.

1933 Proctor and Gamble releases Dreft, the first synthetic detergent.

1971 The 1831 London Bridge reopens in Lake Havasu City, Arizona.

1847 William Lassell discovers Neptune's moon Triton.

1871 After three days of destruction, the Great Chicago Fire ends.

 ## OCTOBER 11

First Lady Nancy Reagan in 1984

1975 *Saturday Night Live* debuts on NBC.

1983 Nancy Reagan introduces her "Just Say No" anti-drug campaign.

2000 NASA launches its 100th space shuttle flight.

1983 The last hand-cranked telephones end service.

1984 Kathryn Sullivan becomes the first American woman to walk in space.

1884 Eleanor Roosevelt is born in New York City.

2017 The Black Swan in Oldstead, North Yorkshire, is named the world's best restaurant.

1996 Ford Motor Company pays $40 million for the right to name Detroit's domed stadium.

 # OCTOBER 12

2012 Pop rock band Imagine Dragons release their hit *Radioactive*.

1869 D.C. Stilson patents the pipe wrench.

1492 Christopher Columbus lands in the Bahamas.

1933 Alcatraz Island in San Francisco becomes a US federal prison.

2015 Dell Computer Company announces plans to buy data storage company EMC for $67 billion.

1892 The Pledge of Allegiance is first recited in schools.

2019 California becomes the first state to ban the sale

and manufacture of new fur products.

1999 The six billionth living human is born.

 # OCTOBER 13

1938 Filming begins for *The Wizard of Oz* in Culver City, California.

1860 James Wallace Black takes the first aerial photo of the U.S. from a balloon.

1792 President George Washington lays the cornerstone for the White House.

2010 The amazing rescue of thirty-three miners trapped in the Copiapo, Chile, mine comes to a close.

1951 The rubber-coated football is used for the first time in Atlanta, Georgia.

2021 Guinness World Records certifies Rumeysa Gelgi from Turkey to be the world's tallest woman at seven feet, seven inches!

1987 The US Navy uses trained dolphins for the first time in military history.

1945 Candymaker Milton Hershey dies at age eighty-eight.

OCTOBER 14

Aerial photographs showing Soviet missile sites in Cuba during the Cuban Missile Crisis

1964 Martin Luther King, Jr. receives the Nobel Peace Prize for advocating non-violence.

1962 The Cuban Missile Crisis begins.

1954 Filming begins on *The Ten Commandments* starring Charlton Heston.

1968 *Apollo 7* gives the first live telecast from a US manned spacecraft.

1971 20,000 Leagues Under the Sea attraction opens at Disney World.

1926 A. A. Milne's book *Winnie the Pooh* is released for sale.

JAN
FEB
MAR
APR
MAY
JUN
JUL
AUG
SEP
OCT
NOV
DEC

JAN
FEB
MAR
APR
MAY
JUN
JUL
AUG
SEP
OCT
NOV
DEC

 # OCTOBER 15

1951 CBS airs the first episode of *I Love Lucy*.

....

2011 Legoland theme park opens in Winter Haven, Florida.

....

1860 Eleven-year-old Grace Bedell writes a letter to Abraham Lincoln to tell him he would look better with a beard.

....

1952 Harper & Brothers publish *Charlotte's Web*.

....

1924 President Coolidge declares the Statue of Liberty to be a national monument.

....

1994 Timothy and Celeste Keys become surviving twins with the longest time between their births (ninety-five days!).

....

1881 The first American fishing journal, the *American Angler*, rolls off the press.

....

President Calvin Coolidge in 1924

OCTOBER 16

1847 Charlotte Brontë publishes her novel *Jane Eyre* in London.

1943 Chicago's first subway station opens.

1998 Jon Postel, a computer scientist and internet developer, dies at age fifty-five.

1869 The Tremont House of Boston becomes the first US hotel with indoor plumbing.

1995 The Skye Bridge opens in Scotland.

OCTOBER 17

1888 The first issue of the *National Geographic* magazine hits newsstands.

1777 US troops defeat the British forces at Saratoga, New York, a turning point in the Revolutionary War.

1989 San Francisco gets hit with a 7.1-magnitude earthquake.

1966 Game show *Hollywood Squares* debuts on NBC.

JAN
FEB
MAR
APR
MAY
JUN
JUL
AUG
SEP
OCT
NOV
DEC

2020 Orkin pest control declares Chicago the "rattiest" city in America.

....

2007 The Dalai Lama receives the US Congressional Gold Medal.

....

1979 Missionary Mother Teresa receives the Nobel Peace Prize.

....

📑 OCTOBER 18

1967 Disney releases *The Jungle Book*.

....

2006 Microsoft releases Internet Explorer 7.

....

1963 Felicette is the first cat to launch into space.

....

1851 Herman Melville publishes his book, *Moby Dick*.

....

1931 American inventor Thomas Edison dies at age eighty-four.

....

1968 The American league grants the Athletics baseball team permission to move to Oakland.

....

1987 Actor Zac Efron is born in San Luis Obispo, California.

....

1926 Queen Marie of Romania becomes the first reigning queen to visit the U.S.

....

OCTOBER 19

Horse-mounted police in present-day New York City

1904 The city of New York begins the service of horse-mounted police.

1953 German monk Michael Stifel predicts the world will end.

1918 Women from the Salvation Army begin making donuts for US soldiers in World War I.

1933 Basketball is added to the Olympic Summer Games.

1987 The stock market faces its largest-ever, one-day crash, with a 22.6% decline.

2009 Amazon releases its international version of the Kindle 2.

1873 Representatives from Columbia,

JAN FEB MAR APR MAY JUN JUL AUG SEP OCT NOV DEC

Princeton, Rutgers, and Yale meet to draft the first football rules.

OCTOBER 20

Pokémon cards in 2020

1996 The first set of Pokémon cards releases to the public.

1922 Lt. Harold R. Harris becomes the first person saved by a parachute.

1708 Construction ends on St. Paul's Cathedral in London.

1818 The 49th Parallel becomes the official boundary between Canada and the U.S.

2009 Astronomers announce the discovery of thirty-two new planets outside our solar system (thousands more are discovered later).

2019 The first nonstop commercial flight from New York to Sydney, Australia, takes off.

1984 The Monterey Bay Aquarium opens its doors in Monterey Bay, California.

1962 *Monster Mash* reaches number one on US music charts.

 # OCTOBER 21

1956 Princess Leia actress Carrie Fisher is born in Beverly Hills, California.

1879 Thomas Edison invents the first practical electric light.

1967 50,000 people join the "March on the Pentagon" to protest US involvement in Vietnam.

1980 The Philadelphia Phillies win their first World Series.

1918 Margaret Owens sets a record for typing on a manual typewriter at a speed of 170 words per minute.

1975 The Coast Guard Academy allows women to enroll.

 JAN
 FEB
 MAR
 APR
 MAY
 JUN
 JUL
AUG
SEP
OCT
NOV
DEC

JAN
FEB
MAR
APR
MAY
JUN
JUL
AUG
SEP
OCT
NOV
DEC

 # OCTOBER 22

1948 The first In-N-Out restaurant opens in Baldwin Park, California.

1746 College of New Jersey, later known as Princeton University, receives its charter.

2012 Singer Garth Brooks joins the Country Music Hall of Fame.

2008 Rock band Imagine Dragons begins.

1995 The United Nations celebrates its fiftieth anniversary.

2016 AT&T purchases Time Warner for $85.4 billion.

2008 Google Play app launches for Android users.

 # OCTOBER 23

1959 Musician-songwriter "Weird Al" Yankovic is born in Downey, California.

1941 Disney's *Dumbo* movie makes its debut.

1994 Robert Bailey makes the longest

Weird Al Yankovic in 2018

NFL punt return–103 yards–while playing for the Rams.

2020 Worcester, Massachusetts, hosts the first US National Womens' Rights convention.

2018 Archaeologists find the oldest intact shipwreck (2,400 years) at the bottom of the Black Sea.

2001 Apple releases the iPod.

1915 Kellerton, Iowa, hosts the first national horseshoe throwing competition.

1930 J. K. Scott wins the first mini-golf tournament in Chattanooga, Tennessee.

OCTOBER 24

JAN
FEB
MAR
APR
MAY
JUN
JUL
AUG
SEP
OCT
NOV
DEC

1901 Daredevil Annie Edson Taylor becomes the first person to go over Niagara Falls in a barrel (and survive).

1992 The Toronto Blue Jays become the first non-US team to win the World Series.

1836 Alonzo D. Phillips patents the friction match.

1949 Construction begins on the United Nations headquarters in New York.

1915 Bob Kane, cartoonist and the creator of *Batman*, is born in New York City.

2005 Civil rights activist Rosa Parks dies at age ninety-two.

1938 Child labor is forbidden in US factories.

OCTOBER 25

2010 Taylor Swift releases her third album, *Speak Now*.

1881 Spanish artist Pablo Picasso is born in Malaga, Spain.

1983 US military invades Grenada.

1955 The first domestic microwaves go on sale.

1972 The FBI graduates its first class of women.

2001 Windows XP operating system debuts.

1962 Author John Steinbeck receives the Nobel Prize for Literature.

1960 The first electric wristwatch goes on sale in New York City.

 # OCTOBER 26

2015 Pentatonics, the a capella group, receives its first top spot on the Billboards 100 chart.

1947 Hillary Rodman Clinton is born in Chicago, Illinois.

2005 Chicago White Sox win their first World Series.

1825 The Erie Canal, connecting the Great Lakes and New York City, officially opens.

1946 *Wheel of Fortune* host Pat Sajak is born in Chicago, Illinois.

1970 *Doonesbury* comic debuts in twenty-eight US newspapers.

1972 The National Park Service begins

JAN
FEB
MAR
APR
MAY
JUN
JUL
AUG
SEP
OCT
NOV
DEC

guided tours of
Alcatraz.

1954 Automaker
Chevrolet introduces
the V-8 engine.

 OCTOBER 27

1904 The New York
City subway system
opens.

1492 Christopher
Columbus finds Cuba.

1925 Fred Waller
receives a patent for
his water skis.

2002 The Anaheim
Angels win their first
World Series.

2019 Governor
Newsome declares a
state of emergency
in California due to
multiple wildfires.

1982 China
announces its
population has
exceeded one billion
people.

1966 *It's the Great
Pumpkin, Charlie
Brown* premieres on
television.

OCTOBER 28

Julia Roberts in 2010

1967 Actress Julia Roberts is born in Smyrna, Georgia.

1955 Bill Gates is born in Seattle, Washington.

1636 Massachusetts Bay colony's Great and General Court founds Harvard University.

1886 President Cleveland dedicates the Statue of Liberty.

1965 The St. Louis Arch is finished.

2020 Scientists discover a new 1,640-foot coral reef at the north end of Australia's Great Barrier Reef.

1954 Author Ernest Hemingway receives the Nobel Prize for Literature.

 OCTOBER 29

JAN
FEB
MAR
APR
MAY
JUN
JUL
AUG
SEP
OCT
NOV
DEC

JAN

FEB
MAR
APR
MAY
JUN
JUL
AUG

1945 The first US-made ballpoint pen goes on sale for $12.50 each.

....

2015 China announces an end to its one-child policy, beginning in 2016.

....

1998 Hurricane Mitch slams into Central America.

....

2014 Microsoft announces its fitness smartwatch, the Microsoft Band.

....

1929 Known as Black Tuesday, the US stock market crashes and the Great Depression begins.

....

1923 "The Charleston" dance craze begins.

....

2018 Nigel Richards wins the World Scrabble Championship for the fourth time.

....

2012 Book publishing giants Penguin and Random House merge.

....

 OCTOBER 30

SEP
OCT
NOV
DEC

2021 Grand Ole Opry broadcasts its 5,000th Saturday night radio program.

....

2003 LeBron James makes his NBA debut with the Cleveland Cavaliers.

....

LeBron James in 2021

1735 John Adams is born in Braintree, Massachusetts.

1894 Daniel Cooper receives a patent for his "Workman's Time Recorder" clock.

1952 Frozen food pioneer Clarence Birdseye sells his first frozen peas.

1943 Canadian hockey player Gus Bodnar scores hockey's fastest first goal in fifteen seconds.

 # OCTOBER 31

1864 Nevada becomes the thirty-sixth state to join the Union.

1860 Girl Scouts' founder, Juliette Gordon Low, is born in Savannah, Georgia.

 JAN
 FEB
 MAR
 APR
 MAY
 JUN
 JUL
 AUG
 SEP
OCT
NOV
DEC

1941 Mount Rushmore National Memorial is completed in Black Hills, South Dakota, after fifteen years of construction.

· ·

1968 President Lyndon B. Johnson announces the end of Vietnam bombing.

· ·

2007 Google shares reach $700 for the first time.

· ·

1517 Martin Luther begins the Protestant Reformation in Germany.

· ·

2020 Actor Sean Connery dies at age ninety.

· ·

2008 Distribution Video Audio, Inc. sends its last-ever shipment of VHS tapes to stores.

· ·

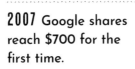

NOVEMBER 1

2002 Disney releases *The Santa Clause 2*.

· ·

1994 Mariah Carey's *Merry Christmas* album debuts and becomes one of the most popular

Christmas albums of all time.

· ·

1962 The first US Christmas stamps go on sale.

· ·

Portrait of John Adams later in life

1800 John Adams becomes the first US President to move into the White House.

· ·

1512 Michaelangelo unveils his work on the Sistine Chapel ceiling.

· ·

1982 Honda becomes the first Asian auto company to manufacture cars in the U.S.

· ·

1848 The Boston Female Medical School, the first medical school for women, opens.

· ·

NOVEMBER 2

2001 *Monsters, Inc.* opens in US theaters.

· ·

2012 Disney's *Wreck-It Ralph* opens in US theaters.

· ·

JAN
FEB
MAR
APR
MAY
JUN
JUL
AUG
SEP
OCT
NOV
DEC

1889 North Dakota becomes the thirty-ninth state to join the Union.

· ·

1889 South Dakota becomes the fortieth state to join the Union.

· ·

1976 Jimmy Carter becomes the thirty-ninth US president.

· ·

1992 Magic Johnson retires from the NBA for the final time.

· ·

2020 *Baby Shark* becomes the most viewed video to date in YouTube history.

· ·

1734 American pioneer and explorer Daniel Boone is born near Reading, Pennsylvania.

· ·

Former President Jimmy Carter volunteers for Habitat for Humanity in 1992

NOVEMBER 3:

1990 *Ice Ice Baby* by Vanilla Ice reaches number one on US music charts.

2016 The Cleveland Indians win the World Series for the first time in 108 years.

2014 New York City opens the One World Trade Center.

1998 Bob Kane, creator of *Batman*, dies at age eighty-three.

1975 *Good Morning America* debuts on ABC.

1952 Frozen bread goes on sale for the first time in a supermarket in Chester, New York.

1998 Researchers announce a newly discovered section of the Great Wall of China.

 # NOVEMBER 4

1980 Ronald Reagan becomes the fortieth US president.

1939 Packard auto manufacturer offers the first air-conditioned car.

2016 DreamWorks Animation releases the movie *Trolls*.

1964 The Easy-Bake Oven makes its debut.

1979 *Jaws* is shown for the first time on television.

1880 James Birch and John Ritty patent the first cash register.

1969 Actor Matthew McConaughey is born in Uvalde, Texas.

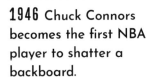

NOVEMBER 5

2004 Pixar's *The Incredibles* opens in US theaters.

1994 George Foreman becomes the oldest heavyweight boxing champion at age forty-five.

1946 Chuck Connors becomes the first NBA player to shatter a backboard.

2007 Google's mobile-phone operating system, Android, debuts.

2013 India launches its Mars Orbiter Mission.

1998 The Beach Boys' single *Kokomo* becomes the week's number-one hit.

2019 China announces gaming regulations for players under eighteen and limits playtime to

JAN
FEB
MAR
APR
MAY
JUN
JUL
AUG
SEP
OCT
NOV
DEC

ninety minutes per
day on weekdays.

NOVEMBER 6

*A statue
honoring
James
Naismith*

1861 James Naismith,
creator of basketball,
is born in Ontario,
Canada.

1973 Coleman Young
becomes Detroit's
first African American
mayor.

1996 NBA great
Michael Jordan scores
fifty points in a game
for the twenty-ninth
time.

1894 William C.
Hooker patents
the spring-loaded
mousetrap.

1850 Charles Henry
Dow, co-founder of

Dow Jones & Co, is born in Connecticut.

1988 Actress Emma Stone is born in Arizona.

NOVEMBER 7

2000 Hilary Clinton becomes the first First Lady to be elected to public office (Senator of New York).

1800 Paris bans women from wearing pants.

2014 Disney's *Big Hero 6* opens in US theaters.

2020 Kamala Harris becomes the first woman and first person of color to be elected as US vice president.

1874 Cartoonist Thomas Nast popularizes the elephant as the symbol of the Republican Party.

US President Zachary Taylor, whose presidency lasted less than a year

1848 Zachary Taylor becomes the twelfth US president.

1973 New Jersey is the first state to allow girls on Little League baseball teams.

1929 New York City's Museum of Modern Art opens its doors.

 # NOVEMBER 8

1895 Wilhelm Roentgen discovers X-rays.

1910 William Frost receives a patent for the first electric bug zapper.

1889 Montana becomes the forty-first state to join the Union.

1837 The first women's college, Mount Holyoke, opens in South Hadley, Massachusetts.

2020 Longtime host of *Jeopardy!* Alex Trebek dies at age eighty.

2016 Americans elect Donald Trump as the forty-fifth US president.

1972 HBO debuts.

2020 California's largest wildfire in state history, the

Camp Fire, begins in
Butte County.

....

📑 NOVEMBER 9

1989 The Berlin Wall
falls, reconnecting the
eastern and western
areas of the city.

....

1922 Albert Einstein
wins the Nobel Prize
for Physics.

....

1848 The state of
California opens its
first US post office in
San Francisco.

....

1994 German
scientists discover
the 110th element,
darmstadtium.

....

2004 Bungie Studios
and Microsoft release

Halo 2 videogame for
the Xbox.

....

2020 The Atlantic
seaboard sets a
record with twenty-
nine storms in one
hurricane season.

....

1944 The Red Cross
receives the Nobel
Peace Prize for its
work during World
War II.

....

1923 The first African
American to win a
gold medal, Alice
Coachman, is born in
Georgia.

....

A group of Sesame Street characters

1969 The first episode of *Sesame Street* airs on PBS.

1951 Area codes are introduced in the U.S.

1983 Bill Gates announces the new Microsoft Windows 1.0 operating system.

1775 The Continental Congress establishes the US Marine Corps.

1911 Andrew Carnegie creates the Carnegie Foundation to further his philanthropic work.

2020 Microsoft releases the Xbox Series X/S.

1970 The Great Wall of China opens to tourists.

1951 The first long-distance phone call

is made without an
operator's assistance.

....

 # NOVEMBER 11

1620 Pilgrims
arrive in Cape Cod,
Massachusetts, after
sixty-six days on the
Mayflower

....

1994 Disney's movie
The Santa Clause
debuts.

....

2008 Taylor Swift
releases her album
Fearless.

....

1918 World War I
comes to an official
end.

....

1889 Washington
becomes the forty-
second state to join
the Union.

....

1921 President
Warren G. Harding
dedicates the Tomb of
the Unknown Soldier.

....

2017 Alibaba, a
Chinese e-commerce
company, sets the
record for largest
single-day sales ever
at $25.3 billion.

....

1926 Historic Route
66 is commissioned.

....

NOVEMBER 12

2019 Disney+ streaming service debuts.

1936 The San Francisco-Oakland Bay Bridge opens.

2018 Comic book legend and *Spiderman* creator Stan Lee dies at age ninety-five.

1971 Arches National Park is established in Utah.

2020 Sony releases the PlayStation 5.

1966 Astronaut takes the first "space selfie."

1990 Computer scientists Timer Berners-Lee and Robert Cailliau propose the idea of the World Wide Web.

Stan Lee in 2017

 NOVEMBER 13

JAN
FEB
MAR
APR
MAY
JUN
JUL
AUG
SEP
OCT
NOV
DEC

1997 Broadway's musical *The Lion King* officially opens.

1940 Disney's *Fantasia* film has its first public screening.

1862 Author Lewis Carroll begins writing *Alice's Adventures in Wonderland*

1927 The Holland Tunnel in New York opens.

2006 Google finalizes a deal to buy YouTube for $1.65 billion in Google stock.

2009 NASA announces that water has been found on the moon.

1942 The US military lowers the minimum draft age from twenty-one to eighteen.

1952 False fingernails are first sold.

Author Lewis Carroll in 1857

NOVEMBER 14

1969 *Apollo 12* successfully launches to the moon.

1948 Price Charles of Wales is born.

1968 Yale University announces it will become a co-ed school.

1983 Michael Jackson's short film *Thriller* debuts in Los Angeles.

2012 *Candy Crush* mobile app game is made available for all smartphones.

1960 At age six, Ruby Bridges becomes the youngest African American student to integrate in the American South.

1915 Booker T. Washington dies at age fifty-nine.

2018 Archaeologists announce the discovery of Tenea, an ancient Greek city near Corinth.

 # NOVEMBER 15

1969 The first Habit Burger Grill opens in Santa Barbara, California.

 JAN
 FEB
MAR
APR
 MAY
JUN
 JUL
AUG
 SEP
OCT
 NOV
DEC

JAN
FEB
MAR
APR
MAY
JUN
JUL
AUG
SEP
OCT
NOV
DEC

1969 The first Wendy's restaurant opens in Columbus, Ohio.

. . . .

1806 Zebulon Pike becomes the first European to see (and later to name) Pikes Peak in Colorado.

. . . .

2011 Mike Krzyzewski records the 903rd win of his NCAA basketball coaching career.

. . . .

2001 Microsoft releases the Xbox gaming console.

. . . .

2013 Sony releases the PlayStation 4 gaming console.

. . . .

1887 American painter Georgia O'Keeffe is born near Sun Prairie, Wisconsin.

. . . .

NOVEMBER 16

1990 *Home Alone* opens in theaters.

. . . .

1907 Oklahoma becomes the forty-sixth state to join the Union.

. . . .

1959 *The Sound of Music* opens on Broadway.

. . . .

1914 The US Federal Reserve Bank in New York City officially opens.

. . . .

The home in Winnetka, Illinois, where Home Alone was filmed

2001 *Harry Potter and the Sorcerer's Stone* opens in theaters.

 **NOVEMBER 17**

2006 Sony Computer Entertainment releases the PlayStation 3.

1871 The National Rifle Association (NRA) receives its first charter from New York.

1800 US Congress holds its first session while the capital building is under construction.

1989 Disney's *Little Mermaid* debuts in US theaters.

1928 The Boston Madison Square Garden (eventually replaced by TD Garden in 1995) opens.

JAN
FEB
MAR
APR
MAY
JUN
JUL
AUG
SEP
OCT
NOV
DEC

JAN
FEB
MAR
APR
MAY
JUN
JUL
AUG
SEP
OCT
NOV
DEC

1982 The Empire State Building is added to the National Register of Historic Places.

2017 The film *Wonder*, based on R. J. Palacio's book, debuts.

1869 The Suez Canal opens in Egypt.

Suez Canal in the present day

 # NOVEMBER 18

1985 Bill Watterson's comic strip, *Calvin and Hobbes*, debuts.

1963 Pushbutton (touch-tone) telephones debut in the U.S.

1928 Walt Disney's *Steamboat Willie* cartoon premieres in New York.

1949 Jackie Robinson becomes the first African American

player to win the MVP.

video game to devices and consoles.

1983 *A Christmas Story* debuts.

2012 Nintendo releases the Wii 2 video game console.

2011 Mojang fully releases its Minecraft

 ## NOVEMBER 19

1980 The first Applebee's restaurant opens in Decatur, Georgia.

1959 Ford Motors ends production of the Edsel car.

2007 Amazon.com begins selling its Kindle electronic reading device.

1942 Fashion designer Calvin Klein is born in Bronx, New York.

1863 President Abraham Lincoln delivers his famous Gettysburg Address.

2018 Rapper Snoop Dog receives his star on Hollywood's Walk of Fame.

JAN
FEB
MAR
APR
MAY

JUN
JUL

AUG

SEP

OCT

NOV
DEC

JAN

FEB

MAR

APR

MAY

JUN

JUL

AUG

SEP

OCT

NOV

DEC

1493 Christopher Columbus finds Puerto Rico.

1965 Kellogg introduces the toaster pastry Pop-Tarts.

NOVEMBER 20

1962 Mickey Mantle receives the American League MVP award for the third time.

1942 US President Joe Biden is born in Scranton, Pennsylvania.

1967 The US population reaches 200 million.

1984 McDonald's makes its 50 billionth hamburger.

1789 New Jersey becomes the first state to ratify the US Bill of Rights.

1973 *A Charlie Brown Thanksgiving* debuts on television.

Windsor Castle, residence of British royal family

1992 Windsor Castle catches fire.

. . . .

 ## NOVEMBER 21

1783 North Carolina becomes the twelfth state to join the Union.

. . . .

2000 Boy band Backstreet Boys releases their album *Black & Blue*.

. . . .

2004 Nintendo releases the DS video game console.

. . . .

2019 Tesla unveils its electric cyber truck.

. . . .

1922 Rebecca Ann Felton of Georgia becomes the first female US Senator.

. . . .

1964 New York's Verrazzano-Narrows Bridge opens to traffic.

. . . .

1960 French author and philosopher Voltaire is born in Paris, France.

. . . .

 ## NOVEMBER 22

1950 The lowest-scoring NBA game ends with the Pistons beating the Lakers 19-18.

2019 Disney releases *Frozen 2* in US theaters.

1842 Mount St. Helens becomes the first modern US volcano to erupt.

1995 Disney releases *Toy Story* in US theaters.

2006 Microsoft's Xbox 360 goes on sale.

1927 Carl J. E. Eliason receives a patent for the snowmobile.

1858 Denver, Colorado, officially becomes a city.

1934 The song *Santa Claus is Comin' to Town* is first heard on the *Eddie Cantor* show.

 # NOVEMBER 23

1936 *LIFE* magazine publishes its first issue.

2016 Disney's *Moana* debuts in US theaters.

1889 San Francisco installs the first jukebox.

1992 American singer and actress

Miley Cyrus is born in Franklin, Tennessee.

1992 IBM introduces its first smartphone, the Simon Personal Computer.

1991 The Sacramento Kings end the longest losing streak in the NBA: 43 games.

1897 John Lee Love receives a patent for the portable pencil sharpener.

1993 The Food Network debuts.

 # NOVEMBER 24

2021 Disney's *Encanto* opens in US theaters.

1877 Anna Sewell publishes *Black Beauty*, the first major animal story in children's literature.

1974 Scientists discover the most complete early human skeleton and name it Lucy.

2009 Donny Osmond wins the ninth season of *Dancing With the Stars*.

1999 Disney's *Toy Story 2* debuts in US theaters.

JAN
FEB
MAR
APR
MAY
JUN
JUL
AUG
SEP
OCT
NOV
DEC

Air Force One lands in Japan

1874 Joseph Glidden receives a patent for barbed wire.

1784 Zachary Taylor, twelfth US president, is born in Orange County, Virginia.

1954 The first US presidential airplane is christened *Air Force One.*

NOVEMBER 25

1867 Alfred Nobel receives a patent for dynamite.

1992 Disney's *Aladdin* debuts in theaters.

1914 Baseball's Joe DiMaggio is born in Martinez, California.

1920 Philadelphia hosts the first Thanksgiving parade.

1940 Woody Woodpecker first appears in a film.

2020 Argentine soccer star Diego Maradona dies at age sixty.

2021 India reports more girls than boys for the first time in its history.

1851 Canada establishes its first YMCA.

 # ⲚⲞⵠⲈⱮⲂⲈⱤ 26

2015 The original *Baby Shark* song uploads to YouTube.

1716 The first African lion in the U.S. goes on display in Boston.

1865 Lewis Carrol publishes *Alice's Adventures in Wonderland*.

1842 Father Edward Sorin founds the University of Notre Dame.

1942 President Franklin D. Roosevelt announces gasoline rationing during World War II.

2018 After a seven-month voyage, NASA's *InSight* lands on Mars.

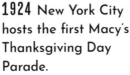

1789 America celebrates its first national Thanksgiving.

⎙ NOVEMBER 27

Tom Turkey, the oldest float in the Macy's parade

1924 New York City hosts the first Macy's Thanksgiving Day Parade.

2013 Disney's *Frozen* debuts in theaters.

1952 CBS begins broadcasting the Macy's Thanksgiving Day Parade.

1960 NHL player Gordie Howe becomes the first to score 1,000 goals.

1755 In South Carolina, Joseph Salvador establishes

the first American
settlement for Jews.

1942 American
musician Jimi Hendrix
is born in Seattle,
Washington.

1885 Ladislaus
Weinek takes the
first photograph of a
meteor.

 # NOVEMBER 28

1929 Ernie Nevers
sets the NFL then-
record for the most
points (40) scored by
a single player.

1922 Skywriting is
used for the first time
as advertising.

1582 William
Shakespeare marries
Anne Hathaway.

1998 Animated
series *Bob the Builder*
premiers in the UK.

1929 Founder of
Motown, Berry Gordon
Jr., is born in Detroit.

1995 The energy-
saving measure of
the 55 miles-per-hour
federal speed limit
officially ends.

1961 Football star
Ernie Davis becomes
the first African
American to win the
Heisman Trophy.

JAN
FEB
MAR
APR
MAY
JUN
JUL
AUG
SEP
OCT
NOV
DEC

1989 Queen Latifah debuts her first album, *All Hail the Queen.*

NOVEMBER 29

A depiction of the original Godzilla

1832 Author Louisa May Alcott, creator of *Little Women,* is born in Germantown, Pennsylvania.

1972 Atari's arcade video game *Pong* debuts.

2001 George Harrison of the Beatles dies at age fifty-eight.

1929 Commander Richard Byrd makes the first flight over the South Pole.

1898 Author C. S. Lewis, creator of The Chronicles of Narnia, is born in Belfast, Ireland.

1961 Enos, the chimpanzee, launches into orbit around the Earth.

2004 Godzilla receives a star on the Hollywood Walk of Fame.

1944 Surgeons at John Hopkins hospital perform the first open-heart surgery.

 # NOVEMBER 30

2017 The world's longest recorded rainbow, lasting nearly nine hours, is seen in Taipei, Taiwan.

1998 Exxon and Mobil oil companies merge, creating Exxon-Mobil.

2004 Ken Jennings loses on *Jeopardy!* after seventy-four consecutive wins.

1858 John Landis Mason receives a patent for the mason jar.

1993 President Bill Clinton signs The Brady Bill, a gun control law.

1872 England and Scotland compete in the first international soccer game.

JAN

FEB
MAR
APR
MAY
JUN
JUL
AUG
SEP
OCT
NOV

DEC

1954 Ann Hodges becomes the first known person to be struck by a meteorite fragment.

1835 American author Mark Twain (Samuel Clemens) is born in Florida, Missouri.

DECEMBER 1

An illustration of Rosa Parks

1955 Rosa Parks refuses to give up her seat on a bus in Montgomery, Alabama.

1914 Ford Motor Company implements the world's first moving assembly line.

1885 Charles Alderton's Dr. Pepper is first served in a drug store in Waco, Texas.

1913 The first drive-in auto service station opens in Pittsburgh, Pennsylvania.

1987 Construction begins on the Channel Tunnel, which would link England and France under the English Channel.

1994 The Game Show Network makes its debut.

 # DECEMBER 2

1982 Dr. Barney Clark receives the first artificial heart transplant.

1970 President Nixon organizes the US Environmental Protection Agency.

1840 Americans elect William Harrison as the ninth US president.

1972 A massive sinkhole named "Golly Hole" opens in Shelby County, Alabama.

1969 Heavyweight boxing champ Muhannad Ali stars in the Broadway musical *Buck White*.

2019 Carissa Moore of Hawaii earns her fourth World Surf League Women's

 JAN
 FEB
 MAR
 APR
 MAY
JUN
 JUL
 AUG
 SEP
OCT
 NOV
DEC

Championship Tour title.

 ## DECEMBER 3

1818 Illinois becomes the twenty-first state to join the Union.

1968 MLB announces that the pitcher's mound will lower from fifteen to ten inches, a move that favors the batter.

2010 Boeing's X-37B successfully returns to earth.

1910 Neon lights are displayed for the first time at an auto show in Paris.

2017 Astronauts on the International Space Station hold the first pizza party in space.

1931 Alka Seltzer is sold for the first time.

1847 Frederick Douglass publishes his first issue of the *North Star* antislavery paper.

 ## DECEMBER 4

A modern-day Burger King in North Carolina

1954 The first Burger King restaurant opens in Miami, Florida.

1843 Manilla paper (like that used in manilla folders and manilla envelopes) receives a patent in Massachusetts.

2021 Indonesia's Mount Semeru erupts.

1881 The *Los Angeles Times* publishes its first edition.

1844 Americans elect James Polk as the eleventh US President

2014 NBC hosts the television special *Peter Pan Live!*

1991 Pan American World Airways ends operations.

1980 Band Led Zeppelin disbands.

 DECEMBER 5

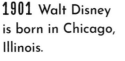

Nelson Mandela in 2006

1901 Walt Disney is born in Chicago, Illinois.

2013 Nelson Mandela dies at age ninety-five.

1848 US President Polk confirms the discovery of gold in California.

1955 The Montgomery Bus Boycott begins.

1854 Topeka, Kansas, officially becomes a city.

1933 Prohibition ends in the U.S.

1792 Americans re-elect Geoge Washington as president.

 DECEMBER 6

1884 Construction is completed on the Washington Monument.

....

1964 Claymation movie *Rudolph the Red-Nosed Reindeer* debuts on NBC.

....

1947 The Florida Everglades becomes a national park.

....

1790 US Congress moves from New York to Philadelphia.

....

2017 President Trump recognizes Jerusalem as the capital of Israel.

....

2017 Starbucks opens its largest cafe in Shanghai, China, measuring the size of half a football field.

....

 # DECEMBER 7

2018 Nintendo's *Super Smash Bros. Ultimate* is released.

....

1941 Japanese launch a surprise attack on US naval base Pearl Harbor.

....

1787 Delaware becomes the first state to join the Union.

....

1972 The first full-color photo of Earth is taken by *Apollo 17*.

....

 JAN

 FEB

 MAR

 APR

 MAY

JUN

 JUL

 AUG

SEP

OCT

NOV

 DEC

1963 Instant replay is used for the first time in football.

1842 The New York Philharmonic presents its first concert.

1909 Leo Baekeland patents Bakelite, the first thermosetting plastic.

📑 DECEMBER 8

2019 Caroll Spinney, who played Big Bird on Sesame Street, dies at age eighty-five.

2004 Women's soccer star Mia Hamm retires from the game.

1998 Finland defeats Sweden in the first women's Olympic hockey game.

1980 Beatles member John Lennon is shot

and killed at age forty.

1857 The first commercial toilet paper hits the market.

2013 Matt Prater kicks the longest field goal in NFL history: sixty-four yards!

1941 President Franklin Roosevelt gives his "Day of Infamy" speech to Congress.

JUN

JUL

AUG

SEP

OCT

NOV

DEC

The surprise attack on Pearl Harbor

1941 The US enters World War II.

 DECEMBER 9

1965 *A Charlie Brown Christmas* premiers on television.

2005 *The Chronicles of Narnia: The Lion, the Witch, and the Wardrobe* opens in US theaters.

1872 P. B. S. Pinchback becomes the first African American governor in Louisiana.

1793 Noah Webster begins New York's first daily newspaper called *American Minerva*.

2019 New Zealand's Whakaari/White Island volcano erupts

JAN FEB MAR APR MAY JUN JUL AUG SEP OCT NOV DEC

1868 The world's first traffic light (gas-powered) is put into service in London.

1992 US Marines arrive in Somalia to begin Operation Restore Hope.

1987 Microsoft releases the Windows 2.0 operating system.

Microsoft Word (version 2.0) on 3.5-inch floppy disks

DECEMBER 10

1817 Mississippi becomes the twentieth state to join the Union.

1901 Theodore Roosevelt becomes the first American recipient of the Nobel Peace Prize.

1830 American poet Emily Dickinson is born in Amherst, Massachusetts.

2007 Argentina elects its first female president, Cristina Fernández de Kirchner.

1948 The United Nations adopts the Universal Declaration of Human Rights.

1967 Otis Redding, the "King of Soul," dies at age twenty-six.

 # DECEMBER 11

2009 Disney's *The Princess and the Frog* debut in theaters.

1816 Indiana becomes the nineteenth state to join the Union.

2010 Nissan of Petaluma delivers the first Nissan Leaf electric car to a customer.

1951 Joe DiMaggio announces his retirement from the MLB.

2009 Rovis Entertainments releases the *Angry Birds* video game.

1991 *Hook* opens in theaters.

2019 Climate activist Greta Thunberg becomes *Time*

JAN
FEB

MAR
APR
MAY
JUN
JUL
AUG
SEP
OCT
NOV

DEC

magazine's "Person of the Year."

1975 First class US postage rises from ten cents to thirteen cents.

 # DECEMBER 12

1899 George Grant receives a patent for the first golf tee.

1787 Pennsylvania becomes the second state to join the Union.

2009 The first episode of *American Ninja Warrior* airs on television.

1986 *Three Amigos* opens in theaters.

1925 The Motel Inn, the world's first motel, opens in San Luis Obispo, California.

1980 Apple launches its initial public offering of stock at $22 a share.

1946 Tide detergent is introduced to the public.

DECEMBER 13

New Zealand coast

1989 Singer-songwriter Taylor Swift is born in West Reading, Pennsylvania.

1928 The clip-on tie is invented in Clinton, Iowa.

2009 Beyoncé's *Single Ladies (Put a Ring On It)* hits number one on Billboard charts.

2019 *Jumanji: The Next Level* debuts in US theaters.

1642 Abel Tasman of the Netherlands discovers New Zealand.

2021 Elon Musk is named *Time* magazine's "Person of the Year."

1769 New Hampshire's Dartmouth College receives its charter.

1967 Musician and actor Jamie Foxx is born in Terrell, Texas.

JAN
FEB
MAR
APR
MAY
JUN
JUL
AUG
SEP
OCT
NOV
DEC

DECEMBER 14

A statue commemorating Roald Amundsen

1911 Norwegian explorer Roald Amundsen reaches the South Pole.

....

1987 The first episode of *Teenage Mutant Ninja Turtles* airs.

....

1972 Astronaut Eugene Cernan becomes the last man to step foot on the moon.

....

2007 *Alvin and the Chipmunks* movie debut in US theaters.

....

1797 George Washington dies at age sixty-seven.

....

1819 Alabama becomes the twenty-second state to join the Union.

....

2016 Amazon announces its first drone delivery.

....

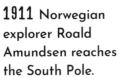

DEC

DECEMBER 15

1966 Walt Disney dies at age sixty-five.

1997 San Francisco 49ers retires the jersey of quarterback Joe Montana.

2001 Italy's Leaning Tower of Pisa reopens after eleven years of stabilization work.

1854 The U.S.'s first street sweeper machine is put into service in Philadelphia.

1979 Chris Haney and Scott Abbott invent the board game *Trivial Pursuit*.

2011 The U.S. formally announces an end to the Iraq War.

1939 *Gone with the Wind* premieres in Atlanta.

 # DECEMBER 16

2020 LeAnn Rimes wins the fourth season on the singing competition show *The Masked Singer*.

1773 The Boston Teaparty takes place at the Boston Harbor.

JAN
FEB
MAR
APR
MAY
JUN
JUL
AUG
SEP
 OCT
 NOV
 DEC

1951 General Electric laboratories produce the first synthetic diamonds.

1775 English author Jane Austen is born in Steventon, England.

1953 The White House holds its first press conference.

1707 Mount Fuji, in Japan, begins its last confirmed eruption.

1950 *Looney Toons* releases its classic cartoon short with Bugs Bunny and Elmer Fudd.

1770 Composer Ludwig van Beethoven is born in the city of Bonn, Germany.

 DECEMBER 17

1903 Wright brothers Orville and Wilbur make their first controlled and powered flight.

1933 Chicago Bears win the first-ever NFL championship.

1948 The original Wright Flyer plane is transferred to the US National Museum at the Smithsonian Institution.

2021 Marvel's *Spider-Man: No Way Home* opens in US theaters.

1790 Excavators in Mexico City discover the Aztec calendar stone.

1777 France formally recognizes the United States as an independent nation.

2021 The first true millipede is found in Australia and has over 1,000 legs!

The Aztec calendar

DECEMBER 18

1946 Film director Steven Spielberg is born in Cincinnati, Ohio.

1787 New Jersey becomes the third state to join the Union.

JAN
FEB
MAR
APR
MAY
JUN
JUL
AUG
SEP
OCT
NOV

DEC

A performance of the Nutcracker Ballet in Ukraine in 2014

2009 James Cameron's film *Avatar* opens in US theaters.

1979 Stanley Barrett breaks the sound barrier driving 739.666 miles per hour.

1943 A ban is placed on sliced bread to conserve wrapping paper materials during World War II.

1892 St. Petersburg, Russia, hosts the first performance of *The Nutcracker* ballet.

1993 Las Vegas's MGM Grand hotel opens its doors.

1936 Su-Lin, the first giant panda in the U.S., arrives in San Francisco from China.

DECEMBER 19

1997 James Cameron's film *Titanic* opens in US theaters.

2012 South Korea elects its first female president, Park Geun-hye.

2004 Tropical Island Resort in Germany becomes the world's largest indoor water park.

1941 Adolph Hitler takes complete command of the German army.

1950 Rose Reid receives a patent for the modern one-piece bathing suit.

1957 Broadway opens its first showing of the musical *The Music Man*.

1918 *Ripleys Believe It or Not!* cartoon premieres in the *New York Globe*.

2008 Ailing automakers General Motors and Chrysler receive rescue loans from the US government.

 # DECEMBER 20

2017 *The Greatest Showman* opens in US theaters.

1946 Holiday film *It's a Wonderful Life* premieres at the

Globe Theater in New York.

2019 President Trump creates the Space Force, a new branch of the US military.

1990 The world's first website and server go live at CERN.

DECEMBER 21

1914 Passport applications require photographs for the first time.

1955 Cardiff becomes the official capital of Wales.

1962 The Osmund Brothers make their debut on the *Andy Williams* show.

1968 American author John Steinbeck dies at age sixty-six.

1812 Jacob and Wilhelm Grimm publish *Grimm's Fairy Tales*.

2012 The music video for *Gangnam Style* becomes the first YouTube video to reach one million views.

1913 The *New York World* newspaper publishes the first modern crossword puzzle.

1971 Bernard Kouchner founds the aid organization Doctors Without Borders.

1891 James Naismith organizes the first basketball game among students.

1898 Marie and Pierre Curie discover the element radium.

1970 Elvis Presley meets President Richard Nixon at the White House.

1948 Actor Samuel Jackson is born in Washington, D.C.

1995 The city of Bethlehem passes from Israeli to Palestinian control.

Marie and Pierre Curie in 1903

 # DECEMBER 22

 JAN
 FEB
 MAR
 APR
 MAY
 JUN
 JUL
 AUG
 SEP
 OCT
NOV
DEC

Anak Krakatoa errupts in 2011

1937 New York's Lincoln Tunnel opens to traffic.

....

1882 Edward Johnson hangs the first electric strand of lights on a Christmas tree.

....

1969 NCAA basketball star Pete Maravich sets a record of 30/31 free throws made in a single game.

....

1956 Colo of the Columbus Zoo in Ohio becomes the first gorilla born in captivity.

....

2018 Part of the Anak Krakatoa volcano falls into the sea, causing a tsunami in Indonesia.

....

1966 The U.S. announces an allocation of 900,000 tons of grain to help alleviate the famine in India.

....

1962 The 100,000,000th point is scored in the NBA.

....

2019 With 144 catches, Michael Thomas breaks the NFL's record for single-season receiving.

DECEMBER 23

1986 *Voyager* aircraft lands after completing the first round-the-world flight without refueling (a nine-day trip).

1815 Jane Austen publishes her novel *Emma*.

2009 *Alvin and the Chipmunks: The Squeakquel* opens in theaters.

1823 The *Troy Sentinel* publishes the poem "The Night Before Christmas" by Clement Moore for the first time.

1997 Phil Jackson of the Chicago Bulls becomes the fastest coach to reach 500 wins.

1975 President Gerald Ford passes the Metric Conversion Act.

DECEMBER 24

1818 The first performance of *Silent Night* is given in a church in Austria.

1777 British explorer James Cook renames Kiritimati Island as "Christmas Island."

1974 Ryan Seacrest is born in Georgia.

1974 Former astronaut John Glenn becomes a US senator for Ohio.

1939 Pope Pius XII makes a Christmas Eve plea for peace during World War II.

1955 The NORAD Santa Tracker begins.

DECEMBER 25

1963 Disney releases its film *The Sword in the Stone*.

1977 British comedic actor Charlie Chaplin dies at age eighty-eight.

1914 During World War I, German and British soldiers hold an unofficial truce to celebrate Christmas.

1821 Clara Barton, founder of the American Red Cross, is born in Oxford, Massachusetts.

1492 The ship of Christopher Columbus,

Illustration of Clara Barton, Red Cross founder

the *Santa Maria*, sinks off the Haitian coast.

2011 Atlanta, Georgia, gets its first snowfall in 128 years.

1997 Jerry Seinfeld announces the last

season of the show *Seinfeld*.

1983 Walt Disney World broadcasts its first live Christmas Day Parade.

📑 DECEMBER 26

1966 The first Kwanzaa celebrations are held in the U.S.

1967 Wham-O receives a patent for

their improvements to the frisbee.

1982 *Time* magazine's "Man of the Year" award goes to the

JAN FEB MAR APR MAY JUN JUL AUG SEP OCT NOV DEC

PC, the personal computer.

1865 James Mason receives a patent for the first US coffee percolator.

2018 Colin O'Brady becomes the first person to ski the 932 miles across Antarctica by himself.

2012 Beijing, China, opens the world's

longest high-speed rail route.

2004 Coastal areas from Thailand to Africa are hit with a devastating tsunami resulting from a 9.3-magnitude earthquake in the Indian Ocean.

1963 The Beatles release their hit single *I Want To Hold Your Hand.*

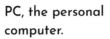

DECEMBER 27

1932 The Radio City Music Hall opens in New York City.

1952 Jimmy Boyd's *I Saw Mommy Kissing Santa Claus* is the

number-one hit of the week.

1822 Chemist Louis Pasteur is born in Dole, France.

Louis Pasteur in 1870

2009 Baking competition show *Cupcake Wars* debuts on the Food Network.

2016 *Star Wars* actress Carrie Fisher dies at age sixty.

1947 Children's show *Howdy Doody* premiers on NBC.

1845 John L. O'Sullivan coins the term "Manifest Destiny" in the *New York Morning News* newspaper.

1923 Eiffel Tower designer Alexandre Gustave Eiffel dies at age ninety-one.

 ## DECEMBER 28

1846 Iowa becomes the twenty-ninth state to join the Union.

1832 John C. Calhoun becomes the first US vice president to resign.

 JAN
FEB
MAR
APR
 MAY
 JUN
 JUL
 AUG
SEP
OCT
NOV
 DEC

1954 Actor Denzel Washington is born in Mount Vernon, New York.

....

1065 Westminster Abbey opens in London.

....

1973 President Nixon signs the Endangered Species Act into law.

....

1996 Italian tenor Andrea Bocelli makes his singing debut at Teatro Romolo Vallif.

....

DECEMBER 29

1851 Thomas Sullivan establishes the first YMCA in America.

....

1845 Texas becomes the twenty-eighth state to join the Union.

....

1848 President James Polk lights the first

gas light in the White House.

....

1982 Dolby introduces surround sound for homes.

....

1862 The modern bowling ball created.

....

DECEMBER 30

1984 LeBron James is born in Akron, Ohio.

....

1963 Game show *Let's Make a Deal* debuts on NBC.

....

1953 RCA sells the first color television sets for $1,175 each.

....

2011 The country of Samoa changes time zones, skipping December 30th altogether.

....

 # DECEMBER 31

1961 The Beach Boys play their first public gig at the Ritchie Valens Memorial Concert in Long Beach.

....

2109 The World Health Organization first hears about "viral pneumonia," later known as COVID-19.

....

1999 The U.S. gives control of the Panama Canal back to Panama.

....

1997 Microsoft announces its purchase of the Hotmail email service.

....

1937 Actor Anthony Hopkins is born in Port Talbot, Wales.

....

1909 The Manhattan Bridge opens, spanning New York City's East River.

....

IMAGE CREDITS

ABOUT THE
AUTHOR

*C*hristin is the author of several books for kids. She lives with her family in California, where she enjoys rollerblading, puzzles, and a good book.

**BUSHEL
& PECK
BOOKS**

ABOUT THE PUBLISHER

*B*ushel & Peck Books is a children's publishing house with a special mission. Through our Book-for-Book Promise™, we donate one book to kids in need for every book we sell. Our beautiful books are given to kids through schools, libraries, local neighborhoods, shelters, nonprofits, and also to many selfless organizations who are working hard to make a difference. So thank you for purchasing this book! Because of you, another book will find itself in the hands of a child who needs it most.

Printed in the United States
by Baker & Taylor Publisher Services